Cults
and the
Occult

Cults and the Occult

REVISED EDITION

EDMOND C. GRUSS

BAKER BOOK HOUSE
Grand Rapids, Michigan 49506

ISBN: 0-8010-3682-8

Printed in the United States of America

Dedicated
to the students
of
Los Angeles Baptist College
Newhall, California

Acknowledgments

The articles in this book were published previously in the *Biblical Research Monthly* (4005 Verdugo Road, Los Angeles, California 90065). My appreciation is expressed to Mr. David L. Cooper, Jr. and his editorial staff for their work in connection with them. Some changes have been made in putting them into the present form.

I also wish to acknowledge indebtedness to the many sources quoted in these pages. Because of the space restrictions placed on the articles I often utilized concise or summary statements by authors of more exhaustive studies on the subjects dealt with. Sources quoted have been identified in the text.

CONTENTS

1

An Introduction to Cults

In the Epistle to the Galatians (1:6-9) the Apostle Paul speaks of the propagation of "another gospel" ("different gospel"—Weymouth)—an actual departure from *the* gospel. The Church Directory in the average newspaper, and the listing under "Churches" in the yellow pages of the phone book, demonstrate the variety of religious ideas and movements in existence today. An examination of the teachings of these groups shows that a number of them actually proclaim "another gospel." A growing number of American religions are commonly identified as "cults" or "sects." While many of these had their beginnings in the nineteenth century, their greatest growth has taken place since 1900, and in many cases, especially since the end of World War II. Commenting on the growth of the cults, Dr. Gordon Lewis stated: "At the dawn of the twentieth century the cults were indistinguishable as a tiny atom, but exploding like atomic bombs the cults have mushroomed upon the American religious horizon" (*Confronting the Cults*, p. 1).

With such organizations as the Jehovah's Witnesses, The Church of Jesus Christ of Latter-day Saints (Mormons) and the Unity School of Christianity numbering membership in the millions, an increasing contact between evangelical Christianity and the cults is inevitable. This alone makes an understanding of the historical backgrounds and theological tenets of these groups imperative for an effective Christian witness.

The Exposure of Error

To expose what is believed to be doctrinal error is often objected to as being negative and as not displaying Christian love. But an examination of the New Testament and the statements of Jesus Christ reveals that the negative is often expressed. Jesus in the Sermon on the Mount warned: "Beware of false prophets, which come to you in sheep's clothing, but inwardly they are ravening wolves. Ye shall know them by their fruits . . ." (Matt. 7:15, 16). It should be noted that the Christian does not judge whether one is, or is not, a false prophet. *Judgment is accomplished by what an individual does and teaches:* "Ye shall know them by their fruits."

In I John 4:1 believers are instructed to "try ['test'—NASB] the spirits whether they are of God: because many false prophets are gone out into the world." Peter warns against "false teachers . . . who . . . bring in damnable heresies, even denying the Lord that bought them . . ." (II Pet. 2:1). In the Galatians passage already cited Paul said of one who preached "another gospel": "Let him be accursed" ("may he be damned!"—Phillips). The reading of Jude 3, 4 yields four important conclusions:

- there is only one faith—"the faith";
- this faith is immutable—"once delivered"; ("once for all delivered"—ASV);
- Christians are to "earnestly contend" for that faith, and
- there are enemies of that faith (v. 4).

Indicating the seriousness of the departure from "the faith" Paul wrote: "Now the Spirit speaketh expressly, that

2

in the latter times some shall depart from the faith, giving heed to seducing spirits, and doctrines of devils [demons—ASV]'' (I Tim. 4:1). That this passage is being fulfilled at the present time is evident as one observes the contemporary scene.

Many other references could be cited, but it is apparent that to expose error, to stand for the truths of the Bible and to insist on a narrowness of doctrine *is* Scriptural. The final authority as to what is doctrinal truth or error must be the Bible.

Cultism Defined

Before the question, What is a *cult?* is answered, it must be realized that although there are many religious movements in the world today, in actuality there are just two. The one finds salvation as a work of man, or man's cooperation with God. The other—true Christianity—attributes salvation to God alone, as that which has been accomplished by God for man (Eph. 2:8, 9; II Tim. 1:9; Tit. 3:5).

What is a cult? Dr. Walter R. Martin, one of the most productive evangelical writers in the cult field, defined cultism as

> *the adherence to major doctrines which are pointedly contradictory to orthodox Christianity,* yet which claim the distinction of either tracing their origin to orthodox sources or of being in essential harmony with those sources. Cultism, in short, is *any major deviation from orthodox Christianity relative to the cardinal doctrines of the Christian faith* [Rise of the Cults, p. 11].

After dealing with the subject, Dr. Lewis concluded:

> A cult, then, is any religious movement which claims the backing of Christ or the Bible, but distorts the central message of Christianity by 1) an additional revelation, and 2) by displacing a fundamental tenet of faith with a secondary matter [Confronting the Cults, p. 4].

Some writers prefer to designate these deviations from

orthodoxy as "sects" as has been done by Dr. John H. Gerstner in his book, *The Theology of the Major Sects*. In dealing with the word, Gerstner explained that "evangelicals generally use 'sect' when referring to those Christian denominations not regarded as evangelical" (p. 9). The standard of being regarded as "evangelical" is adherence to the fundamental doctrines of biblical orthodoxy, with the Person and work of Christ as the key areas. While the terms "cult" and "sect" are almost synonymous, the latter word has a wider application.

Dr. Anthony Hoekema's treatment on "The Distinctive Traits of the Cult" is helpful.

> In setting forth what I believe to be the distinctive traits of the cult, I do not wish to give the impression that not the slightest trace of these characteristics is to be found in the churches. If we are honest with ourselves, we shall find vestiges of these characteristics in the churches, too. I venture to affirm, however, that the traits which will now be described are so uniquely characteristic of the cult that any group in which they play a leading role can no longer be recognized as belonging to the true church of Jesus Christ [*The Four Major Cults*, pp. 377, 378].

The distinctive traits of the cult are then given and discussed: 1)"An Extra-Scriptural Source of Authority"; 2) "The Denial of Justification by Grace Alone"; 3) "The Devaluation of Christ"; 4) "The Group as the Exclusive Community of the Saved"; 5) "The Group's Central Role in Eschatology" (*The Four Major Cults*, pp. 378-403). These characteristics are specifically applied to Christian Science, Jehovah's Witnesses, Mormonism and Seventh-day Adventism.

An important question which relates to the "cult" or "evangelical" classification has been raging concerning the status of the Seventh-day Adventists. In recent years the Adventists have contended that they should be viewed as evangelical, but evangelical scholars have split in their acceptance of this claim. For example, of the authors already cited in this discussion, Martin concluded that the Seventh-day Adventists should not be viewed as a cult (*The Kingdom of the Cults,* p. 360), while Lewis, Gerstner and Hoekema identified them as non-evangelical (*Confronting the Cults,* pp. 124, 125; *The Theology of the Major Sects,* p. 10; *The Four Major Cults,* pp. 388-403). It should be added that the present writer agrees with the latter conclusion, but along with these men, he would not place Adventism in the same class as the Jehovah's Witnesses, Mormons or Christian Scientists. In conclusion on this point, J. K. Van Baalen is quoted:

> . . . the writer regrets to state that a renewed study of the tenets and the methods of S.D.A. has accentuated rather than lessened his conviction that S.D.A.— although its adherents are clearly sincere, and many Christians are among them—as a movement is dangerous [*The Chaos of the Cults,* 4th rev. ed., p. 250].

The Current Scene

It is impossible to accurately state how many new cults have appeared in recent years, but informed observers estimate "anywhere from 2,500 to as high as 5,000" (*L.A. Times,* December 1, 1978, p. 1). In a survey of the current religious scene it becomes obvious that an expanded definition of what constitutes a cult must be employed.

In his helpful article, "What is a Cult?" Brooks Alexander presents the problem and suggests an approach.

> What is a "cult"? Ten or twenty years ago, this would have been an easy question to answer; today the guidelines have become somewhat muddled.
> . . . The problem is that neither a definition based on a standard of Christian orthodoxy, nor one based on techniques of behavioral manipulation and conditioning is comprehensive enough to cover all the ground.
> . . . Perhaps the best approach is one which combines

the two different standards without confusing them [*SCP Newsletter,* Jan.-Feb. 1979].

Included in the theological designation of what constitutes a cult are such characteristics as "a false or inadequate basis of salvation" and a "false basis of authority." Most of the non-theological standards for identifying a cult, Alexander states, pertain to techniques used in gaining and training converts, and include: "isolation or 'involvement' of the recruit to the point that the group controls all of the incoming information," "economic exploitation or an enslaving organizational structure," and "esotericism" by which he means "a deliberately created gap between the truth about the cults which is given to the 'inner circle' and a misleading image which is projected to the public at large."

David Breese's book, *Know the Marks of Cults* presents a good survey and expansion of the approach mentioned by Alexander.

The Existence and Growth of Cults

How does one account for the existence of cults? Why do cults thrive? It must be recognized that there are two forces (powers) in the universe which oppose each other. These are led by God on the one side and the opposer of Heaven, Satan, on the other. Satan's goal is to blind men to the gospel of Christ, to deceive the world and to receive worship for himself (Matt. 4:9; II Cor. 4:4; Rev. 12:9). One of Satan's most effective tools is the propagation of false doctrine. Second Corinthians 11:13-15 warns that Satan disguises himself as "an angel of light" and his human representatives as "apostles of Christ" and "ministers of righteousness."

Why do cults thrive? Many answers have been suggested: the enlisting of large numbers of laymen; the use of home doctrinal studies; the skillful methods of making converts; the use of the mass media; the publication and distribution of large quantities of attractive literature; the strong financial support; the efforts to meet human needs; the exploitation of the uncertainty of the times. All of these suggestions help to explain cultism's growth, but there is yet another important point which relates to the Church. Walter Martin succinctly states the problem:

> . . . it is vitally essential that we understand one of the basic causes of cultism: *the unfortunate failure of the church to institute and emphasize a definite, systematic plan of cult evangelism and apologetic and doctrinal theology.* The average Christian is, sad to say, terribly unprepared to defend his faith thoroughly. In a word, he knows *what* he believes, but too often he does not know *why* [*Rise of the Cults,* p. 14].

Conclusion

The proliferation and activity of the cults present a real challenge to those who are true believers in Christ and the Word of God. For years the cults have confronted the Church. It is now time that the *cults were confronted* as never before **by the evangelical Church!**

A SELECTIVE BIBLIOGRAPHY OF GENERAL WORKS ON THE CULTS

Alexander, Brooks, "What is a Cult?" *Spiritual Counterfeits Project Newsletter,* Jan.-Feb. 1979.

Beck, Hubert F. *How to Respond to the Cults.* St. Louis: Concordia Publishing House, 1977.

Breese, Dave. *Know the Marks of Cults.* Wheaton: Victor Books, 1975.

Burrell, Maurice C. and Wright, J. Stafford. *Whom Then Can We Believe?* American ed. 1976; Chicago: Moody Press, 1976.

Enroth, Ronald. *The Lure of the Cults.* Chappaqua: Christian Herald Books, 1979.

Gerstner, John H. *The Theology of the Major Sects.* Grand Rapids: Baker Book House, 1960.

Hoekema, Anthony A. *The Four Major Cults: Christian*

Science, Jehovah's Witnesses, Mormonism, Seventh-day Adventism. Grand Rapids: Wm. B. Eerdmans Publishing Co., 1963.

Lewis, Gordon R. *Confronting the Cults*. Philadelphia: Presbyterian and Reformed Publishing Co., 1966.

Martin, Walter R. *The Kingdom of the Cults*. Rev. ed., 1968; Minneapolis: Bethany Fellowship, Inc., 1965.

————. *Rise of the Cults*. Santa Ana., Calif.: Vision House, 1977.

Spittler, Russell P. *Cults and Isms: Twenty Alternates to Evangelical Christianity*. Grand Rapids: Baker Book House, 1962.

Van Baalen, J. K. *The Chaos of Cults*. 4th rev. ed.; Grand Rapids: Wm. B. Eerdmans Publishing Co., 1962.

2
Jehovah's Witnesses

In 1957 Marcus Bach identified the Jehovah's Witnesses as "the fastest-growing religious movement in the world" (*Christian Century,* 2/13/57, p. 197). But this observation was no longer true in 1977 and 1978, as the Witnesses' Service Year Report showed active worldwide membership losses of 1 percent and 1.4 percent. Statistics for the United States indicated a 3 percent loss for both years. By the end of 1978 worldwide membership was just under 2.2 million. That the outreach and influence of this organization greatly exceeds its membership becomes evident from the circulation figures of the magazines and books published by the Watchtower Bible and Tract Society, Brooklyn, New York, the governing body of the Jehovah's Witnesses.

The work of the Witnesses among nominal Christians, new converts and on the mission fields, has caused a great deal of confusion and heartache. This is the case because this cult denies most of the major doctrines accepted by evangelical Christians.

This brief survey can only present a few highlights concerning the Witnesses' history, doctrines, publications and program. The study is concluded with some suggestions on dealing with the adherents of this cult and their doctrinal views. An Annotated Selective Bibliography presents materials for further study and distribution.

History

The history of the Witnesses is conveniently divided into three periods which coincide with the three presidents which have led the movement.

• **Charles T. Russel** (1852-1916) founded *Zion's Watch Tower*—now *The Watchtower*—in 1879 and Zion's Watch Tower Tract Society in 1884 (later renamed). In addition to his speaking and editorial work Russell penned six volumes titled *Studies in the Scriptures* (originally *Millennial Dawn*), which appeared between 1886 and 1904. By the time of his death in 1916, the legal and doctrinal foundation of the Society had been established.

• **"Judge" Joseph F. Rutherford** (1869-1942), the second president—under whose leadership the name "Jehovah's Witnesses" was taken in 1931—was a prolific writer. In addition to his speaking and editorial work, and the publication of dozens of booklets, he wrote an average of one new book each year. A number of doctrinal and Scriptural reinterpretations marked his administration. Rutherford became the "new oracle of God's message for this age" and Russell's writings and interpretations were often neglected or rejected as not abreast of progressive light. By 1938 the independent ecclesiae of Russell's day were brought under the "Theocratic" control—subservient to the Society's headquarters in Brooklyn.

• **Nathan H. Knorr** (1905-1977)—following Rutherford's death in 1942—officially took over the leadership of the Witnesses, a movement then slightly over 115,000. Knorr demonstrated his organizational ability in that great growth took place under his direction in the areas of membership, outreach, buildings and publications. Vice-president Frederick W. Franz succeeded Knorr.

(The details of the history of the Jehovah's Witnesses are found in the books by Gruss, Hoekema, Martin, Rogerson and Schnell—all listed in the Bibliography. The Society's biased account of its own history is found in *Jehovah's Witnesses in the Divine Purpose*.)

Doctrines

The easiest way to treat the doctrinal system of this cult is to present its denials of evangelical Christianity. Other characteristic doctrines are also stated.

Doctrinal denials include the : 1) denial of the Trinity; 2) denial of the deity of Christ (Arian view); 3) denial of the Personality of the Holy Spirit (viewed as "God's active force"); 4) denial of man's immortal soul (It should be noted that Scripturally "immortality" applies to man's future body. Orthodoxy uses immortality as a term to explain that man's soul or spirit continues to exist after death.); 5) denial of the Biblical view of the Atonement (Christ's death is viewed by the Witnesses as that of only a perfect *man* and as a "corresponding ransom"); 6) denial of the bodily resurrection of Christ (the Witnesses teach that He arose a spirit creature and materialized bodies on various occasions in order to be seen by His disciples); 7) denial of salvation by faith; 8) denial of salvation outside their organization; 9) denial of the "born again" experience for all (this experience—they say—is just for 144,000 of the Witnesses); 10) denial of the eternal punishment of the lost (claiming annihilation is their fate); 11) denial of the bodily, visible return of Christ (Christ "returned" invisibly in 1914 and there was an invisible "rapture" in 1918).

Other characteristic doctrines: 1) the Bible cannot be understood today without the Society; 2) blood transfusion is rejected—if a Witness received one willingly it would result in his eternal death; 3) Witnesses refuse to serve in the military and to salute the flag—to salute the flag is an act of idolatry; 4) holidays and celebrations, such as Christmas,

Easter and birthdays, are rejected as pagan in origin; 5) the present gathering of the Jews to Palestine is not a fulfillment of prophecy. Israel has been set aside and God's promises are being realized in "spiritual Israel," the Jehovah's Witnesses.

Publications

The printed page has been one of the most effective tools of the Witnesses. Their two semi-monthly magazines, *The Watchtower* and *Awake!,* had publication figures (for each issue in January 1980) of 8.75 and 7.65 million, respectively. *The Watchtower* magazine is the "theological" publication of the Society. The publication of one or more books each year, with first editions of one to five million copies, has a real impact.

The New World Translation of the Holy Scriptures was completed in 1961. Dr. Hoekema agrees with what many others have said concerning this version:

> . . . Their *New World* Translation is by no means an objective rendering of the sacred text into modern English, *but is a biased translation in which many of the peculiar teachings of the Watchtower Society are smuggled into the text of the Bible itself* [Anthony A. Hoekema, *The Four Major Cults,* pp. 238, 239].

The Witnesses also have two Greek interlinear New Testament texts. The older work is *The Emphatic Diaglott,* translated by Benjamin Wilson, a Christadelphian. *The Kingdom Interlinear Translation of the Greek Scriptures,* published in 1969, combines the Westcott and Hort Greek text with the Society's translation and an improved text of the *New World Translation.* Both works clearly reveal a doctrinal bias. Two topically arranged Bible-verse handbooks (with verses frequently out of context) should be mentioned: *Make Sure of All Things* (1953) and *Make Sure of All Things; Hold Fast to What is Fine* (1965). A Bible dictionary, *Aid to Bible Under-*

standing, which reflects the Witnesses' understanding on many of the topics explained, was completed in 1971. A Jehovah's Witness can now ¡"study" the Bible and never leave Watchtower Society publications.

Program

All movements have a program of some kind to bring in the converts. It was William Schnell, author of *Thirty Years a Watch Tower Slave,* who clearly explained the Witnesses' "seven-step program." 1) Get literature into the hands of the people through house-to-house or other outreach. 2) Follow up with a "back call" to determine and encourage interest. 3) Try and arrange a "book study," using the Society's latest books. 4) Get the person showing interest to come to the congregational "book study." 5) Bring those showing interest to the "Watchtower study." 6) Encourage attendance at the "Service meeting" and the "Theocratic School." These two meetings train the Witnesses in their outreach program. 7) The last step is the dedication of the life to Jehovah in baptism.

In the steps presented above, the reader will notice the absence of a definite time of being "born again"—an experience only for the 144,000 according to the Society.

Dealing With the Witnesses

The individual Witness: 1) He is trained in a particular doctrinal system. 2) He is committed to the Society without reservations as "God's channel." 3) He is "brainwashed," a fact attested to by many former Witnesses. 4) He normally rejects being "born again"; therefore, he cannot give a testimony of an accomplished personal salvation.

Dealing with the Witness: 1) Do not argue. 2) Don't get sidetracked. 3) Deal only with primary doctrines: the Person and Work of Christ are vital. 4) Give your personal testimony of salvation. 5) Don't deal with the Witness without your

Bible. 6) Pray that he will be saved.

(Other suggestions on the subject are included in the 4-page tract, "Dealing with Jehovah's Witnesses," available from this writer.)

Selected References

- **The Trinity:** Matt. 3:16, 17; 28:19; John 14:26; 15:26; I Cor. 12:3-6; II Cor. 13:4; Eph. 2:18; 3:1-5, 14-17; 4:4-6; 5:18-20; I Pet. 1:2; Jude 20, 21.
- **The Deity of Christ:** Isa. 9:6 (cf. Isa. 10:21); John 1:1, 23 (cf. Isa. 40:3); John 8:58; 12:37-41 (cf. Isa. 6:1-10); Heb. 1:1-12 (cf. Ps. 102:25-27); Rev. 22:13 (see the "Deity of Christ" article in the Bibliography).
- **The Personality of the Holy Spirit:** Matt. 28:19; John 14:26; 16:13; Acts 10:19, 20; Rom. 8:26, 27; I Cor. 12:11.
- **The bodily resurrection of Christ:** Ps. 16:9, 10 (cf. Acts 2:25-31); Mark 16:6; Luke 24:3-8 (cf. John 2:19-22); Luke 24:36-43; Rom. 8:11; I Cor. 15:15.
- **Salvation by faith:** Rom. 4:5; 5:8-11; Eph. 2:8-10; II Tim. 1:9; Tit. 3:4-8; I John 5:11-13.
- **Born Again:** I John 5:1-5; John 3:3, 5, 7 (See Luke 13:28, 29 and Matt. 8:11. Old Testament saints will be found in the "kingdom of God" or "kingdom of heaven.")
- **The soul** (spirit): Acts 2:27; I Thess. 5:23; Heb. 12:23; Rev. 6:9-11; 20:4.
- **Eternal punishment:** Matt. 25:46; II Pet. 2:17; Jude 13; Rev. 19:20 with 20:10. The Greek word *basanidzo*, "to torment" (Rev. 20:10, in every place where it appears in the N.T., speaks of pain and conscious suffering (cf. Mark 5:7; Luke 8:28; II Pet. 2:8; Rev. 9:5; 12:2).
- **The visible return of Christ:** Zech. 12:10; Matt. 23:39; 24:30; Acts 1:11; I Thess. 4:16, 17; Rev. 1:7.
- **The message of the early Church in Acts:** 2:22-40; 3:13-26; 4:2, 10-12, 33; 5:30-32, 42; 8:4-6, 35; 9:20; 10:39-43; 11:20, 26; 13:28-41; 16:30-32; 17:2-4, 18, 31; 18:5; 19:13; 20:21; 24:24; 26:22, 23.

AN ANNOTATED SELECTIVE BIBLIOGRAPHY OF MATERIALS FOR FURTHER STUDY

Dencher, Ted. *Why I Left Jehovah's Witnesses*. Fort Washington, Pa.: Christian Literature Crusade, 1966. Presents the writer's testimony and a Scriptural refutation of several key Witness doctrines.

Gruss, Edmond C. *Apostles of Denial: An Examination and Exposé of the History, Doctrines and Claims of the Jehovah's Witnesses*. Nutley, N. J.: Presbyterian and Reformed Publishing Co., 1970. A 324-page book which deals with Witnesses in a comprehensive way.

———. *The Jehovah's Witnesses and Prophetic Speculation*. 2nd ed.; Nutley, N. J.: Presbyterian and Reformed Publishing Co., 1975. Presents an examination and refutation of the Witnesses' position on the second "coming" of Christ in 1914, Armageddon, and the "end of the world." Covers the 1975 prediction and failure.

———. *We Left Jehovah's Witnesses—A Non-Prophet Organization*. Nutley, N. J.: Presbyterian and Reformed Publishing Co., 1974. The book features the personal testimonies of six couples who left the Jehovah's Witnesses and why many have identified the group as a non-prophet organization—a false prophet.

Hoekema, Anthony A. *Jehovah's Witnesses*. Grand Rapids: Wm. B. Eerdmans Publishing Co, 1963. This book is an updated portion of material appearing in *The Four Major Cults* (Eerdmans, 1963). A scholarly presentation of the Witnesses' theology and a refutation of their denials on the Deity of Christ and eternal punishment.

Martin, Walter R. and Klann, Norman H. *Jehovah of the Watchtower*. Rev. ed., 1974; Chicago: Moody Press, 1974. A comprehensive treatment of the subject.

Rogerson, Alan. *Millions Now Living Will Never Die*. London: Constable & Co. Ltd., 1969. Contains a good treatment of the history of the movement.

Schnell, William J. *Thirty Years a Watch Tower Slave*. Grand Rapids: Baker Book House, 1956. Contains the author's experiences and his interpretation of the inner workings of the Society.

Thomas, F. W. *Masters of Deception*. Grand Rapids: Baker Book House, 1972. Examines and refutes the Witnesses' major doctrinal errors. Contains a helpful scriptural index.

Publications distributed by the Department of Apologetics, Los Angeles Baptist College, P.O. Box 878, Newhall, Calif. 91322.

Books:

Apostles of Denial: An Examination and Exposé of the History, Doctrines and Claims of the Jehovah's Witnesses. $5.50 postpaid.

The Jehovah's Witnesses and Prophetic Speculation. $2.95 postpaid.

We Left Jehovah's Witnesses. $3.50 postpaid.

Tracts and Articles:

"Why a Witness of Jesus Christ—Not a Jehovah's Witness?"

"Jehovah's Witnesses: The Watchtower Society and Prophetic Speculation"

"Dealing with Jehovah's Witnesses"

"Is the Watchtower Society God's Channel?"

"The Deity of Christ" (8-page reprint of an article by F. F. Bruce and W. J. Martin; also in booklet form) ($2.00 for 8 copies postpaid)

All tracts are 8½ × 11 folded and are $3.50 per 100 postpaid. Lots of 100 may be mixed titles. A book order will include a sample of each of the tracts currently available.

Three organizations with extensive literature ministries to Jehovah's Witnesses and for Christian outreach are:

Witness Inc., P.O. Box 597, Clayton, Calif. 94517

Missionary Crusader, 4606 Avenue H., Lubbock, Tex. 79404

Help Jesus, P.O. Box 265, Whittier, Calif. 90608. Help Jesus is a worldwide ministry with representatives in many states and foreign countries. The National Director in the U.S. may be contacted at the following address: Help Jesus, Box 690, Colton, Calif. 92324.

3

The Latter-day Saints (Mormons)

On April 6, 1830, Joseph Smith, Jr. (1805-1844) founded the "Church of Christ" (the original name) with six charter members at Fayette, New York. In 1978 membership had climbed to 4.1 million. This growth has been explained by some observers as the result of three main factors: 1) missionaries, 2) money, and 3) magnificence. One does not have to look far to find each of these factors illustrated in the Church of Jesus Christ of Latter-day Saints. For example, in 1978 there were over 27,000 missionaries serving the LDS Church.

Mormons, and sometimes professing evangelical Christians, frequently criticize those who view and expose the Mormon Church as *a non-Christian cult*. To such criticism it should be pointed out that the initial attack was not launched by orthodoxy, but rather by the founder of Mormonism, Joseph Smith. *Joseph Smith's Testimony*, written in 1838 and currently published and distributed by the LDS Church, relates the following:

> My object in going to inquire of the Lord was to know which of all the sects was right, that I might know which to join. . . .

I was answered that I must join none of them, for they were all wrong and the Personage who addressed me said that all their creeds were an abomination in His sight; that those professors were all corrupt; that "they draw near to me with their lips, but their hearts are far from me; they teach for doctrines the commandments of men, having a form of godliness, but they deny the power thereof."

He again forbad me to join any of them. . .[p.5].

The Mormons view their church as the "restored" church of Jesus Christ and all other professing Christian groups as being apostate. This is illustrated in *A Uniform System for Teaching Investigators,* a booklet once used by Mormon missionaries in their proselyting work, where the potential convert is led to say concerning other churches and his own: "They are false. . . . *There was a complete apostasy and my church is false*" (p. 18). Since the beginning of this movement, and still today, the issue is clear: either orthodox Christianity is "false" or Mormonism is, there can be no "peaceful coexistence" on this matter.

Because of the extent and complexity of the subject only several key areas are surveyed. To enhance the value of this brief survey there is an annotated list of materials for further study and information as to where materials on Mormonism may be obtained.

Mormonism as a System

The Lutheran theologian, F. E. Mayer, concluded:

As a religious system Mormonism is a mixture of theosophy, spiritism, and elements of paganism, under a thin veneer of Christian terminology. As a philosophy it is slightly materialistic and approaches Islam [*The Religious Bodies of America,* 4th ed., p. 462].

The heart of Mormon theology, according to Mayer,

teaches that man, an eternally preexistent soul, is placed upon earth in order to gain "the remission of his sins"

18

through obedience to the laws and regulations laid down by the priesthood and ultimately that he reaches perfection by a continual advance and eternal progress. In the interest of this central doctrine the Mormons have developed their theology and worship [p. 458].

These expressions indicate that many non-Christian sources and teachings are embodied in the Mormon system.

The Sources of Mormon Doctrine

Mormonism finds doctrinal authority in five sources.

• *The King James Version* of the Bible is accepted as "the word of God as far as it is translated correctly . . ." (*Articles of Faith*—art. 8). In 1831 Joseph Smith began a revision of the *King James Version*. (There is evidence that the work was completed in 1833.) This revision has been published by the Reorganized LDS Church and is designated the *Inspired Version*.

• It is claimed that *The Book of Mormon* presents God's dealings with the Western continent, just as the Bible presents God's dealings with the Eastern continent.

• *Doctrine and Covenants* is important as a source of some of the distinctive doctrines of Mormonism, such as: celestial marriage and baptism for the dead.

• *The Pearl of Great Price* is a compilation of several writings: *The Book of Moses, The Book of Abraham,* a portion of Smith's translation of the Bible (Matt. 24), a portion of *Joseph Smith's Testimony,* and *The Articles of Faith.*

The above four major sources are designated the "Standard Works."

• Further revelations through the leadership of the Church have become the fifth source of doctrinal authority. Brigham Young University professor, C. C. Riddle, quoting a Church authority, wrote: "He said that the most important scriptures that the Church has today are the words of President McKay [presently S. W. Kimball]. And they are scripture" (*Lectures on Jesus Christ*, p. 3).

The following quotations from Mormon writers indicate that the Bible is subordinated: "Whenever any discrepancies were found between the *Book of Mormon* text and the Bible account, Joseph Smith followed the *Book of Mormon* and thereby set an example to the Church" (Wm. E. Berrett, *Teachings of the Book of Mormon*, p. 5). Joseph Fielding Smith stated: "Guided by the *Book of Mormon, Doctrine and Covenants,* and the Spirit of the Lord, it is not difficult for one to discern the errors in the Bible" (*Doctrines of Salvation,* III, p. 191).

Mormon Doctrine

Mormon doctrine is quite complex but a summary under several major areas of theology should suffice.

God: The Trinity is rejected and the three Persons of the Godhead are viewed as separate and distinct. God the Father has a body of flesh and bones and the Holy Spirit is a personage of Spirit. Joseph Smith stated: "God was once as we are now, and is an exalted man and sits enthroned in yonder heavens! . . . He was once a man like us. . . ." (Joseph Fielding Smith (ed.), *Teachings of the Prophet Joseph Smith,* pp. 345, 346). There is a plurality of Gods.

Man: Before men inhabit the earth they exist as spirits. Man was "created" in the physical image of God. The Garden of Eden was located in Independence, Mo. The *Fall* is interpreted as that which accomplished good. Original sin is rejected.

Christ: The difference between other men and Christ is one of degree—not kind. The Scriptural teaching on the Virgin Birth is rejected. Brigham Young stated: ". . . Jesus Christ was not begotten by the Holy Ghost" (*Millennial Star,* XV, p. 770). Christ's birth was the result of a union

20

between God the Father and Mary. Jesus was a polygamist (*Journal of Discourses*, II, pp. 81, 82). Christ's death guarantees that all will be resurrected. Individual salvation is gained by the person in the degree to which he believes and obeys the Mormon gospel. Some sins are said to be beyond the blood atonement of Christ. In *Mormon Doctrine*, Bruce McConkie wrote that "There are some serious sins for which the cleansing blood of Christ does not operate, and the law of God is that men must have their own blood shed to atone for their sins . . ." (p. 87). (See the detailed discussion of blood atonement in *Mormonism—Shadow or Reality?*, pp. 175-188.)

Church and Ordinances: It is believed that God's Church entered into apostasy and remained in that state until 1830. The true Church was reestablished with the restoration of the Aaronic and Melchizedek priesthoods (conferred upon Joseph Smith and Oliver Cowdery). Baptism is absolutely necessary for salvation. Baptism for the dead is performed (based upon I Cor. 15:29). The Lord's Supper is administered weekly and water is used.

Eschatology: Before Christ returns to rule over Zion and Jerusalem there are three "gatherings": 1) The Ephraimites—Mormons—to Zion (strictly speaking, Independence, Mo.); 2) The Jews—to Palestine; 3) The Lost Ten Tribes—to Zion. There is a one-stage advent, with a resurrection at the beginning of the millennium—the "first Resurrection." Those raised are the believing dead and those who had not heard the Gospel. The wicked are burned up and suffer punishment in preparation for the postmillennial period. Satan is bound and there is peace on the earth. The wicked are raised after the millennium (1,000 years). Satan has his last fling and some follow him in defeat. The "saved" spend eternity in one of three kingdoms, designated: Celestial, Terrestrial and Telestial. There is opportunity for advancement within each.

A helpful survey of Mormon theology is *A Study of the Articles of Faith*, by James E. Talmage (before his death one of the Twelve Apostles of the Church). The *Articles of Faith* set forth the basic doctrines of the LDS as written by Joseph Smith in 13 articles. They are included in *The Pearl of Great Price*. An excellent presentation of Mormon doctrine by a non-Mormon scholar is that by Anthony A. Hoekema in *Mormonism*.

Mormon Doctrine and its Refutation

The gist of some major Mormon doctrines or denials is given below and appropriate Bible and other references in refutation are cited.

- **Plurality of Gods:** Isa. 43:10,11; 44:6, 8; James 2:19. (Also see the *Book of Mormon*, Alma 11:27-29.)
- **God an exalted man:** Num. 23:19; Mal. 3:6; John 4:24 (cf. Luke 24:39); Rom. 1:22, 23.
- **Preexistence of man:** Gen. 2:7 indicates that man experienced his creation on earth. Christ was preexistent, but there is no mention of man's preexistence.
- **The fall was "a blessing in disguise"** (stated by Joseph Fielding Smith, *Doctrines of Salvation*, I, p. 114): Rom. 5:12-21; 8:19-22.
- **Rejection of original sin:** Ps. 51:5; Rom. 5:12-21; Eph. 2:1-3.
- **Rejection of the Virgin Birth:** Matt. 1:18-20; Luke 1:26-35.
- **Rejection of Salvation by grace through faith alone:** Rom. 3:21-30; Eph. 2:8-10.
- **Some sins are beyond the blood of Christ (blood atonement):** I John 1:7-9.
- **The church went into apostasy and required restoration:** It is denied that the apostasy was universal and therefore a restoration was not required: Matt. 16:18; I Tim. 4:1, "some shall depart from the faith" (not "all").
- **The Aaronic and Melchizedek priesthoods were restored:** Heb. 7:12, 24; I Pet. 2:9; Rev. 1:5, 6. Every

believer becomes a priest through redemption. Christ alone is our great High Priest (Heb. 9:24-26). The word "unchangeable" in Heb. 7:24 means that "which passeth not from one to another"—it is the peculiar possession of Jesus Christ: "His priesthood is untransferable"— *Goodspeed*. (See the study, *Latter-Day Saints—Where Did You Get Your Authority?* by Hal Hougey.)

- **Joseph Smith is a Prophet of God:** See *The Testing of Joseph Smith, Jr.—Was He a Prophet?* by James D. Bales. "Fifty-eight prophecies of Joseph Smith examined in detail by G. T. Harrison failed to come to pass." (Gordon R. Lewis, *The Bible, the Christian, and Latter-day Saints*, p. 18). Joseph Smith certainly failed the test of Deut. 18:20-22.

- **The restored Gospel is Mormonism:** Paul warns of "another gospel" (Gal. 1:8, 9).

AN ANNOTATED SELECTIVE BIBLIOGRAPHY OF MATERIALS FOR FURTHER STUDY

Brodie, Fawn M. *No Man Knows My History*. 2nd ed., 1971; New York; Alfred A. Knopf, 1945. The best biography on Joseph Smith, written by the niece of the late president of the LDS Church, David O. McKay. It resulted in her excommunication from the church for heresy.

Cowan, Marvin W. *Mormon Claims Answered*. Salt Lake City: Marvin W. Cowan, 1975. Packed with useful information this volume is "an attempt to analyze some of the basic Mormon claims in the light of the Bible and authoritative Mormon sources" (Intro.).

Fraser, Gordon H. *Is Mormonism Christian?* Chicago: Moody Press, 1977. A consolidation of two of Frazer's earlier works which deals with Mormon doctrine, practice, teaching and history. Compares Mormon doctrine with Biblical Christianity.

————. *Joseph and the Golden Plates: A Close Look at The Book of Mormon*. Gordon H. Fraser, 1978. The *Book of Mormon* compared with known anthropological and archaeological facts.

Hoekema, Anthony A. *Mormonism*. Grand Rapids: Wm. B. Eerdmans Publishing Co., 1963. Presents a concise treatment of Mormon history, source of authority and doctrines. An appendix examines the genuineness of the *Book of Mormon*.

Martin, Walter R. *The Maze of Mormonism*. Santa Ana, Calif.: Vision House Publishers, 1979. This is a good overall treatment which is a thorough revision and updating of a previous work.

Smith, John L. *Brigham Smith*. Clearfield, Utah: The Utah Evangel Press, 1969. An historical novel which gives a clear insight into Mormonism and the Mormon. An interesting presentation.

Tanner, Jerald and Sandra. *Mormonism—Shadow or Reality?* Salt Lake City: Modern Microfilm Company, 1972 ed. (In January 1980 Moody Press released a condensed and updated version of this book under the title of *The Changing World of Mormonism*.) The Tanners have written several dozen works—this is one of their best. It is recommended that the reader obtain the "Book List" from the address below.

Turner, Wallace. *The Mormon Establishment*. Boston: Houghton Mifflin Co., 1966. An excellent book by a correspondent for the *New York Times*. Deals with many controversial issues.

Whalen, William J. *The Latter-day Saints in the Modern World*. Notre Dame, Ind.: University of Notre Dame Press, 1964. An excellent book by a Catholic layman which deals with many controversial issues.

For Bibliographies listing works both pro and con on Mormonism see: *Mormonism* by Hoekema, pp. 95-101; *The Theology of the Major Sects* by Gerstner, pp. 195, 196, and *No Man Knows My History* by Brodie, pp. 489-499.

Materials

Tracts, pamphlets, cassettes and books for study and distribution may be obtained from the following:

• Utah Missions, Inc., Box 47, Marlow, Okla. 73055

- Utah Christian Tract Society, P. O. Box 725, La Mesa, Calif. 92041
- Wally Tope, Box 1100, La Canada-Flintridge, Calif. 91011.
- CARIS, P. O. Box 1783, Santa Ana, Calif. 92702.
- The Christian Research Inst., Box 500, San Juan Capistrano, Calif. 92675.
- Ex-Mormons for Jesus, P. O. Box 1322, Garden Grove, Calif. 92642. (This address is just one of many EMFJ branches in the US and Canada.)
- Modern Microfilm Co., P. O. Box 1884, Salt Lake City, Utah 84110. Modern Microfilm, run by the Tanners, publishes and handles a good selection of materials dealing with Mormonism. Ask for their "Book List" and a free subscription to *The Salt Lake City Messenger*.
- Department of Apologetics, Los Angeles Baptist College, P. O. Box 878, Newhall, Calif. 91322. A special selection of materials on Mormonism is available for $2.00 postpaid.

4

Christian Science

The Church of Christ, Scientist, founded by Mrs. Mary Baker Eddy in the last quarter of the nineteenth century, has presented a challenge to orthodox Christianity in its theology and stress on healing. Many have left denominational churches to become Christian Scientists because of a "healing" experience. The membership of this movement is not available because its *Church Manual* instructs: "Christian Scientists shall not report for publication the number of the members of The Mother Church, nor that of the branch churches" (Article VIII, Sect. 28—1911 ed.). Some writers have calculated a following in excess of one million, but the current following is by other estimates only about twenty-five percent of that, and the number of churches and Christian Science practitioners (spiritual counselors) have been in decline for a number of years (*L.A. Times,* October 31, 1976, Part 2, pp. 1, 5; January 16, 1978, Part 2, p. 4). It has been estimated that approximately eighty percent of Scientist members are found in the United States and that seventy-five percent are women. This last statistic has caused some writers to dub the organization "the cult of the American ladies."

In the survey of Christian Science which follows limited

attention is given to: its founder; its use of censorship and doctrine. A selective Bibliography concludes the study.

The Founder of Christian Science

It is important to gain some acquaintance with Mrs. Mary Baker Eddy, for apart from her Christian Science would not exist. Mary Baker was born in Bow, New Hampshire in 1821. Her family was devoutly religious and she grew up with an orthodox Congregational Church background. In *Retrospection and Introspection* Mrs. Eddy explained how she reacted against the Reformed faith, and in particular, the doctrine of predestination (pp. 13-15). Her childhood was

> marked continually by a strange illness which seemed to grow in severity with Mary's increasing years. Young Mary, history tells us, was quieted during these fits by rocking in a specially built cradle made of an old sofa where she remained until she fell asleep. As a small child she had often been subject to frequent fits evidenced by a peculiar physical lethargy erupting into violent spasms of pronounced hysteria and ending eventually in unconsciousness. Mary Baker was also plagued with a neurotic temper which exhibited itself whenever her wishes were denied and her anger aroused [Martin and Klann, *The Christian Science Myth,* pp. 18, 19].

Her personal problems, emotional and physical, continued beyond her youth and help to explain the emphasis of her religion on the healing of mind and body.

Mary Baker was married three times. Her first husband, George Glover, died shortly before the birth of their only child. Her second marriage was to Dr. Daniel Patterson, a dentist; this ended in a divorce, she being the innocent party. Her third husband, Asa Eddy, died of a chronic heart condition, but Mrs. Eddy claimed that he had been killed by "mesmeric poison" (Dakin, *Mrs. Eddy,* pp. 166-168).

The turning point in Mrs. Eddy's life began in 1862 when she became a patient and student of Quimby [P.P.

27

Quimby of Portland, Maine was the founder of mental healing in America]. Then, in the ten years following that healer's death (1866), she compounded his system of mental therapeutics with an idealistic metaphysics and a pantheistic theology to create a distinctive creed, summarized in a brief doctrinal formula known as the "Scientific statement of being." "There is no life, truth, intelligence, or substance in matter. All is infinite Mind and its infinite manifestation, for God is All in all, Spirit is immortal Truth; matter is mortal error. Spirit is the real and eternal; matter is the unreal and temporal. Spirit is God, and man is His image and likeness; hence, man is spiritual and not material."

Consequently, "the only reality of sin, sickness, or death is the awful fact that unrealities seem real to human, erring belief . . ." [Raymond J. Cunningham, "The Impact of Christian Science on the American Churches, 1880-1910," *The American Historical Review,* April, 1967, p. 886].

Other key dates in the life of Mrs. Eddy and the development of Christian Science include:

- 1866 She claimed that as a result of a serious fall on a slippery walk (Feb. 1, 1866) she discovered the principles of Christian Science (*Science and Health,* p. 107, lines 1-6). Her account of the severity of the accident was contradicted by the attending physician, Dr. Alvin Cushing in an affidavit of over a thousand words (*Mrs. Eddy,* pp. 60-62).
- 1875 The publication of the first edition of *Science and Health* (*with Key to the Scriptures* was added in 1883). The present edition has been revised, rewritten, polished grammatically and structurally; this in spite of the fact that Mrs. Eddy claimed divine inspiration:

  I should blush to write of *Science and Health with Key to the Scriptures* as I have, were it of human origin and I apart from God its author, but as I was only a scribe echoing the harmonies of heaven in divine metaphysics, I cannot be super-modest of the Christian Science textbook [*Christian Science Journal,* Jan., 1901, cited in *The Christian Science Myth,* p. 55].

28

- 1879 The Church of Christ, Scientist was organized in Charlestown, Massachusetts. This became The First Church of Christ, Scientist, in Boston—the Mother Church—in 1892.
- 1895 The *Church Manual* was published. It established the permanent procedures of the government of the Church. Christian Science is a highly authoritarian organization because of this publication, for it states: "This Manual shall not be revised without the written consent of its author" (Article XXXV, Sect. 1; see also Sect. 3—1911 ed.).
- 1910 Mrs. Eddy "passed on" December 3, 1910. Since her death the leadership of the movement has been in the hands of a self-perpetuating Board of Directors.

Christian Science Censorship

The authors of *The Christian Science Myth* felt the subject of censorship was so significant that an entire chapter was devoted to it (chapter 7). It was described as "one of the most distinguishing characteristics of the Christian Science religion . . ." (p. 132). The appearance of a chapter from this book in the January, 1955 *Eternity* magazine and the subsequent publication of the entire exposé brought Christian Science opposition. (See chapter 9 in the Dec., 1955 edition of the book.)

The most well-known attempt at censorship concerns the publication of the book *Mrs. Eddy: The Biography of a Virginal Mind* by Edwin F. Dakin in 1929. (See *The Christian Science Myth*, pp. 143-149.)

Other writers have also recognized the power of the Christian Science Committee on Publication. Lutheran author, George Wittmer wrote: "The powerful forces of Christian Science censorship have been marshaled again and again to suppress writings that were unfavorable to the cause of this sect" (*Christian Science in the Light of the Bible*, p. 23). Catholic journalist, William J. Whalen observed: "In recent years the Committee's methods of boycott and intimidation have managed to stifle nearly all published criticism of the cult" (*Separated Brethren*, p. 191). In conclusion, the present writer's own experience is cited. When he was scheduled to speak on Christian Science at a nearby church a notice was sent to the local Christian Science branch. This notice was forwarded to the area Committee on Publication, which responded with a letter, which stated in part:

> I am surprised to hear that anyone would feel that he is serving the Cause of Christianity (so badly needed in the world today) by an "Affrontal Attack," as is expressed, on someone else's religious point of view.

Christian Science Doctrine

In the limited space available it is impossible to properly present Christian Science doctrine with appropriate documentation. Therefore the following quotations are taken from the conclusions reached by Anthony Hoekema in his book, *The Four Major Cults*. His study is based on primary sources and the interested reader should check this source for the reasons behind the conclusions.

- **The Bible:**

Science and Health declares the Bible to be our sufficient guide to eternal life" (p. 497), but as Hoekema comments:

> In actual practice, however, Christian Scientists accept the Bible only as interpreted by Mrs. Eddy, whose book, *Science and Health* . . . is really their ultimate source of authority, and is thus placed above the Bible [p. 182. See also pp. 183-186].

- **God:**

God, to the Christian Scientist, is divine Mind, and Mind is all that truly exists. . . . Christian Science repudiates the orthodox Trinity [pp. 189, 190].

- **Man:**

Christian Science, in its anthropology, denies the reality of the body, of sin and the fall, and repudiates man's temporality and finiteness [p. 200].

- **Jesus Christ:**
Christian Science denies the unity of the Person of Jesus Christ, Jesus' present existence, the absolute necessity for Jesus' earthly mission, the incarnation of Christ, the virgin birth of Jesus, the sinlessness of Jesus, the full deity of Jesus, and Jesus' genuine humanity. In addition, they reject Jesus' suffering, death, physical resurrection, and ascension into heaven [p. 207].

It is clear that Christian Scientists repudiate the teaching which is the heart of the gospel: that Jesus Christ suffered and died on the cross in order to bear the burden of God's wrath against sin, so that we might be saved through His blood. We are left with a Jesus who was merely an example [p. 209].

- **Salvation:**
For Christian Science salvation from sin is accomplished when one ceases to sin, or when one stops believing that there is such a thing as sin. In either event, the death of Christ has nothing to do with salvation; if Christ had never existed, it would have made no real difference [p. 212].

- **Eschatology:**
Christian Science repudiates every major tenet of Christain eschatology [p. 221].

Hoekema concludes that Christian Scientists reject every major doctrine of historic Christianity and then he states:

> Christian Scientists, therefore, have no more right to apply to themselves the title *Christian* than have Buddhists or Hindus—with whose teachings, indeed, Christian Science has greater affinity than with those of Christianity. We conclude that, strictly speaking, Christian Science is neither Christian nor science [p. 221].

Conclusion

A refutation of Christian Science doctrine has not been

included in this study because the natural, normal interpretation of the Bible, as well as common sense, are a complete exposé. It must be admitted that Mrs. Eddy did have some unusual talents and that she built one of the most powerful churches in America. But as the Bible and the biographies of Milmine and Dakin clearly show, she was not a trustworthy channel of divine revelation. First Timothy 4:7 seems very appropriate: "But refuse profane and old wives' fables. . . ."

AN ANNOTATED SELECTIVE BIBLIOGRAPHY OF MATERIALS FOR FURTHER STUDY

Bates, Ernest S. and Dittemore, John V. *Mary Baker Eddy, the Truth and the Tradition*. New York: Alfred A. Knopf, 1932. Of this book Martin and Klann write:

> A work so devastating in its documentary evidence, and so unimpeachable in its source that Christian Scientists today do not even care to admit its existence [*The Christian Science Myth*, p. 35].

Dakin, Edwin Franden. *Mrs. Eddy, the Biography of a Virginal Mind*. New York: Charles Scribner's Sons, 1929. A masterful biography which Christian Scientists tried to suppress. See the story on this in *The Christian Science Myth*. Reprinted in recent years by Grosset and Dunlap.

Gottschalk, Stephen. *The Emergence of Christian Science in American Religious Life*. Berkeley: Univ. of California Press, 1973. A comprehensive and scholarly interpretation of the development of Christian Science by a member.

Hoekema, Anthony A. *The Four Major Cults*. Grand Rapids: Wm. B. Eerdmans Publishing Co., 1963 (pp. 171-221). This section is also published as a separate book. Contains an excellent development of Christian Science theology based on primary sources.

Martin, Walter R. and Klann, Norman H. *The Christian Science Myth*. Revised edition, Dec., 1955. Grand Rapids: Zondervan Publishing House, 1955. An able treatment dealing with Christian Science history, doctrines, censorship and cures. Includes a refutation of their theology. The edition listed contains some additional material.

Milmine, Georgine. *The Life of Mary Baker G. Eddy and the History of Christian Science*. 2nd ed., 1971; Grand Rapids: Baker Book House, 1909 (copyright renewed 1937). Originally a series of articles which appeared in *McClure's* magazine in 1907 and 1908 and published in book form in 1909. The one printing quickly disappeared. It is a masterful job of research. In the introduction to this second edition, published by Baker, Elizabeth Shepley is quoted as she discussed the mystery of the book.

> The book that followed the magazine serial disappeared almost immediately from circulation—the Christian Scientists are said to have bought the copies. It is hard to find one nowadays, even in a big library, and the reader is likely to have to borrow the only copy from the chief librarian's safe, and be watched by a detective while reading it (xv).

An excellent bibliography is included in *The Four Major Cults* (pp. 424-431). Two other helpful bibliographies are found in *The Christian Science Myth* and Dakin's *Mrs. Eddy*. In correspondence with the Christian Science Committees on Publication in Boston, the following books were recommended for background study: *Science and Health with Key to the Scriptures* (Eddy); *Historical Sketches* (Smith); *Mary Baker Eddy and Her Books* (Orcutt); *A Century of Christian Science Healing: The Christian Science Way of Life* (John); *Why I Am a Christian Scientist* (Leishman); *Christian Science: Its Encounter with American Culture* (Peel).

In 1977 a group calling itself The Association of Former Christian Scientists, Born Again, prepared and distributed a 9-page letter to Christian Scientists. The letter lists Todd B. Ehrenborg as Director and John R. Warren as President. The address: 1550 S. Anaheim Blvd., Anaheim, Calif. 92805.

Another ministry to reach Christian Scientists and those in other of the Mind Sciences is Christian Way, Carolyn Poole director (P. O. Box 1675, Lancaster, Calif. 93534).

The July 20, 1979 issue of *Christianity Today* (pp. 36, 37) surveys the current situation in the Christian Science Church.

5

Unity School of Christianity (Unity)

The Unity School of Christianity, founded by Myrtle and Charles Fillmore in the 1880's, has become one of the best-known healing cults of American origin. Unity claims a following of over two million members and it has been characterized as "the largest mail order religious concern in the world . . ." (Walter R. Martin, *Unity,* Preface). The impressive headquarters of this movement is located in Unity Village, a 1200-acre development near Lee's Summit, Missouri.

In the brief treatment which follows, Unity's history, outreach and doctrines are surveyed. The cult is then viewed and evaluated in the light of the Bible and orthodox Christian scholarship. A brief bibliography concludes this study.

History

The Unity story began in Kansas City, Missouri, when in 1886 Myrtle and Charles Fillmore attended a lecture given by Dr. Eugene B. Weeks. He represented the Illinois Metaphysical College, founded by Emma Curtis Hopkins, a former associate with Mrs. Mary Baker Eddy and an editor of the

Christian Science Journal (James D. Freeman, *The Household of Faith*, p. 42). Myrtle had suffered for years with tuberculosis and malaria and "from her earliest childhood, she had been taught to think of herself as an invalid" (ibid., p. 39). Of the ideas presented by Dr. Weeks, one stood out in Myrtle Fillmore's mind: " '*I am a child of God and therefore I do not inherit sickness*' " (ibid., p. 44). According to her own testimony her entire life changed with the acceptance of this statement and in two years she was "no longer an invalid" (ibid., p. 49). The story of her healing is set forth in *How I Found Health*.

Charles Fillmore, who had been a cripple from youth as a result of a skating accident (ibid., p. 22), also applied the healing principles discovered by his wife. He saw results and wrote: " 'My chronic pains ceased. My hip healed and grew stronger, and my leg lengthened until in a few years I dispensed with the steel extension that I had worn since a child' " (ibid., p. 55).

The Fillmores wanted to share their new-found faith with others and in 1889 the first issue of *Modern Thought* was published. Their religious philosophy was clearly stated in the following: "We see the good in all religions and we want everyone to feel free to find the Truth for himself wherever he may be led to find it" (ibid., p. 42). In developing their religious system the Fillmores were extremely eclectic, a fact which will be developed later. In the spring of 1891, the term "Unity" was taken as the name of the organization. This name was aptly chosen, for it embodies the central principle of the group: "Unity of the soul with God, unity of all life, unity of all relgions, unity of the spirit, soul and body; unity of all men in the heart of the truth" (Marcus Bach, *They Have Found a Faith*, p. 223).

Because of his dislike for dogma it was thirty years before Charles Fillmore was induced to write a statement of faith. But even then he cautioned:

We are hereby giving warning that we shall not be bound by this tentative statement of what Unity believes. We may change our mind tomorrow on some of the points, and if we do, we shall feel free to make a new statement.

Myrtle Fillmore died in 1931 and Charles married Cora G. Dedrick, who had served as private secretary to him and his wife. He died in 1948. The great growth of Unity was largely due to the Fillmores' two sons, Lowell and Rickert, who became president and secretary respectively. Growth of the movement may also be attributed to the emphasis on health and prosperity.

Outreach

The Unity program is worldwide. " 'Unity literature goes into every country of the world, Russia and its satellite nations excepted' is the statement that has been made many times. This statement is literally true" (James A. Decker, ed., *Unity's Seventy Years of Faith and Works*, p. 100). "The Unity Printing Department is one of the largest and best equipped in the Midwest" (ibid., p. 93). One of the important aspects of the literature work is the publication of five periodicals: *Unity, Daily Word, New, Wee Wisdom,* and *Weekly Unity.* All are high quality, attractive publications.

Information made available in the early 1960's indicated that annually Unity published more than fifty books and booklets, printed sixty million pieces of literature, and handled 600,000 requests for prayer. Mail averaged 7,000 letters a day. In addition Unity has a correspondence school and other programs are conducted at Unity Village. A recent issue of *Weekly Unity* lists the addresses of hundreds of Unity Centers and Classes, most of which are in the United States, but a number are abroad.

An extensive radio and TV schedule is also maintained. "The Word," a one-minute inspirational thought message, is being aired over hundreds of radio stations, and a number of television stations as well. Unity's outreach cannot be ignored.

Doctrines

That the Fillmores were eclectic in formulating Unity's doctrinal system has already been mentioned. Charles Ferguson was right when he stated that Unity "was undoubtedly joined by an umbilical cord to New Thought, and sired by Christian Science" (*The Confusion of Tongues*, p. 217). All three stress healing, but there are a number of differences also. While recognizing these, Van Baalen states: "We maintain, however, that they are as much alike as triplets" (*The Chaos of Cults*, 4th rev. ed., p. 134. See the discussion, pp. 133-137).

Reflecting on its eclectic nature, F. E. Mayer concluded that:

> Unity has elements of Quakerism (inner light), of Christian Science (healing), of Theosophy (reincarnation), of Rosicrucianism (cosmic unity), of Spiritism (the astral or physical self), of Hinduism (idealism) [*The Religious Bodies of America*, 4th ed., p. 545].

Since space does not allow the quotation and examination of Unity's doctrinal position, the summary by Gordon Lewis, after such examination, is cited. He concludes that this cult differs from orthodox Christianity in at least seven essential respects:

- **The Bible is not divine revelation,** but merely fallible human witness to revelation. It may be reinterpreted at will in accord with Fillmore's flashes of insight.
- **Man's primary problem** is not sin before a holy God, but mistakes in thinking. So man's primary need is not for the gospel of redemption but examples of denials and affirmations.
- **Jesus is not God** incarnate but a man who effectively demonstrated the Christ ideal.

- **Jesus made no real atonement** at Calvary for man's sin but exemplified the power of mind over matter.
- **Christ's resurrection was no miracle** but another demonstration of thought control.
- **Faith is a magic wand** which uses divine principle to satisfy personal desires.
- **In place of divine grace** through faith alone Unity stresses human striving to overcome the lower by the higher self [*Confronting the Cults,* p. 156].

In addition, one other important teaching of this cult should be mentioned:

- **The doctrine of reincarnation:**

  We believe that the dissolution of spirit, soul, and body—caused by death—is annulled by rebirth of the same spirit and soul in another body here on earth. We believe the repeated incarnations of man to be a merciful provision of our loving Father to the end that all may have opportunity to attain immortality through regeneration, as did Jesus. "This corruptible must put on incorruption" [Article 22 of *Unity's Statement of Faith*].

Scripture's answer to reincarnation is clear:

- **. . . It is appointed unto men once to die, and after this** *cometh* **judgment** [Heb. 9:27];
- Therefore, as through one man sin entered into the world, and death through sin; and so death passed unto all men, for that all sinned [Rom. 5:12];
- We are of good courage, I say, and are willing rather to be absent from the body, and to be at home with the Lord [II Cor. 5:8];
- For me to live is Christ, and to die is gain. But if to live in the flesh—*if* this shall bring fruit from my work, then what I shall choose I know not. But I am in a strait betwixt the two, having the desire to depart and be with Christ; for it is very far better [Phil. 1:21-23];
- For we know him that said, Vengeance belongeth unto me, I will recompense. And again, The Lord shall judge his

people. It is a fearful thing to fall into the hands of the living God [Heb. 10:30, 31—ASV].

Evaluation

A number of evangelical writers and theologians have written on the Unity School of Christianity and what it would mean to accept this cult's teachings. Two of these conclusions are cited.

J. Oswald Sanders wrote:

> We would say that the greatest danger in this movement lies in the many beautiful and true sentiments contained in its literature which would appeal to the uninstructed, leading them to believe that they are imbibing true Scripture teaching. Satan does his most dangerous work when he is masquerading as an angel of light.

> With an impersonal God, a Christ degraded to the level of man, and man elevated to deity, with a denial of sin and consequent emasculation of the atonement, with self-regeneration and the Hindu doctrine of reincarnation, we are amazed at the temerity of its promoters in designating it a school of "Christianity" [*Heresies: Ancient and Modern,* p. 61].

Walter R. Martin concluded:

> In order to join the Unity School of Christianity (the Unity cult), it must be understood that one would have to renounce every basic doctrine of the Christian faith, deny the deity, physical resurrection and personal coming of our Lord, and believe in the reincarnation of the soul as over against the doctrine of the physical resurrection of the body [*Unity,* p. 31].

Similar conclusions have been reached by *every* evangelical scholar who has written on the subject.

Conclusion

With Unity, as with Christian Science, the refutation of the system is given by a natural, normal interpretation of the

Bible. In dealing with adherents of the Unity School of Christianity it is necessary to define terms which are employed. It is also important that the following doctrines be stressed:

- that God is a Person, not a Principle;
- that man is a lost, depraved and helpless sinner in need of God's grace for salvation, and
- that redemption as set forth in the Bible is vastly different from that propagated by Unity.

Pertinent are these words from the pen of the Apostle John:

> Beloved, believe not every spirit, but prove the spirits, whether they are of God; because many false prophets are gone out into the world [I John 4:1].

SELECTIVE BIBLIOGRAPHY

There are no books and only a few booklets (many out of print) which have been written by evangelical scholars exclusively on the Unity School of Christianity. Most treatments are included in books which deal with a number of cults. The Unity School of Christianity materials are voluminous and easy to obtain from the cult itself or from public libraries.

Examination and Refutation of Unity

Griffin, Nancy H. *What Says "Unity"? What Says God?* Los Angeles: American Prophetic League, n.d. A 24-page booklet comparing Unity and the Bible.

Lewis, Gordon R. *Confronting the Cults*. Philadelphia: Presbyterian and Reformed Publishing Co., 1966. Unity treated, pp. 131-161.

Martin, Walter R. *The Kingdom of the Cults*. Minneapolis: Bethany Fellowship, Inc., 1965. Unity treated, pp. 275-294.

————. *Unity*. Grand Rapids: Zondervan Publishing House, 1957. A 32-page booklet dealing with history, doctrines and refutation.

Talbot, Louis T. *What's Wrong with Unity School of Christianity?* Findlay, Ohio: Dunham Publishing Co., 1956. A 64-page booklet dealing with history, doctrines and refutation. Compiled from a four-part series which appeared in *The King's Business*, October, 1955–January 1956.

————. "What's Wrong with the Unity School of Christianity?" *The King's Business*, June, 1961, pp. 19-22.

Van Baalen, Jan Karel. *The Chaos of Cults*. 4th rev. ed.; Grand Rapids: Wm. B. Eerdmans Publishing Co., 1962. Unity treated, pp. 128-145.

Whalen, William J. *Unity School of Christianity*. Claretian Publications, 1966. A booklet by a Catholic journalist.

Unity Materials

On a visit to Unity Village during the summer of 1971 the following Unity books were recommended to the writer as basic for an introduction to Unity.

Lessons in Truth (Cady), *Christian Healing and Dynamics for Living* (C. Fillmore), *What are You?* (Shanklin).

The book *The Household of Faith (The Story of Unity)*, by James D. Freeman and the booklets *The Adventure Called Unity* and *Unity's Statement of Faith* are also helpful.

6

Herbert W. Armstrong and the Worldwide Church of God

This writer first became aware of Herbert W. Armstrong and the Radio Church of God (The Worldwide Church of God since 1968) shortly after World War II through listening to "The World Tomorrow" broadcast. It was estimated that this radio program (when Armstrong's son, Garner Ted, was the speaker) had the potential to be heard by 95 percent of the population of America and Canada (Leslie K. Tarr, *Moody Monthly,* Sept., 1972, p. 24), and in addition, it reached all the continents of the world.

From listening to the program it was first concluded that Armstrong belonged in the doctrinal camp of the Jehovah's Witnesses. Later it was learned that his theological system was far more complex. In his article, "Herbert Armstrong: Mr. Confusion," Roger Campbell expressed the typical experience and conclusion of many writers on the subject:

> After being asked about Herbert Armstrong, I set out to identify him. I soon discovered, however, that pigeon-holing this fellow's teaching was no simple task. Just

when I thought I had him labeled with one of the well-known cults, another of his teachings would come to my attention that would divorce him from that group. Here was sort of an hybrid-heretic who seemingly had jumped the fences of three or four mistaken groups to take along some peculiar and unscriptural doctrine of theirs to make it his own [*The King's Business*, Feb., 1962, p. 24].

While the discerning Christian will soon realize that much of Armstrong's message is less than orthodox, unfortunately many who are contacted by his ministry do not have this discernment and confusion results.

What is the history of the Worldwide Church of God and its founder? What is its appeal? What are its major doctrines and are they scriptural? These and other points are dealt with in this study. A bibliography is featured for further study.

History

Herbert W. Armstrong was born in Des Moines, Iowa in 1892. Although he "was brought up in a respectable Protestant church of traditional Christianity" (*The Plain Truth*, Feb., 1973, p. 1), his early years were characterized by a basic disinterest in religion. At the age of eighteen, after graduation from high school, he began a career in public relations and advertising. He married Loma Dillon in 1917. The Armstrongs moved to the Pacific Northwest, and in 1926 Herbert was motivated to study the Bible through the influence of his wife who began observing the seventh-day Sabbath. She had been brought to this position by Mrs. Ora Runcorn, a family friend, who was a member of the Church of God (Stanberry, Mo.), "an early offshoot of the Seventh-day Adventist Church" (Harry Lowe, *Radio Church of God*, pp. 18, 19). After investigation Mr. Armstrong also was "converted" and began keeping the Sabbath. He later identified himself with the Church of God and was ordained in 1931.

43

When doctrinal disputes rent the Church of God, a sizable portion of the membership withdrew and set up a new headquarters in Salem, West Virginia in 1933. Armstrong joined this faction, but afterward broke from it and established his own work, the Radio Church of God.

A radio ministry began in January, 1934 over 100-watt station KORE, Eugene, Oregon. The first issues of *The Plain Truth* were also run the same year on a borrowed mimeograph. The events of 1934 are seen as having great prophetic import:

> . . . What was actually happening, back in 1934, was precisely this: Jesus Christ (Rev. 3:8) was opening the gigantic mass-media DOOR of radio and the printing press for the proclaiming of His same original GOSPEL to all the world! [*The Autobiography of Herbert W. Armstrong,* I, p. 503]

In *A True History of the True Church,* Herman L. Hoeh explained the importance of Herbert W. Armstrong to God's program today:

> Jesus chose Paul, who was highly educated, for spreading the gospel to the Gentiles. He later raised up Peter Waldo, a successful businessman, to keep His truth alive during the Middle Ages. In these last days, WHEN THE GOSPEL MUST GO AROUND THE WORLD, Jesus chose a man amply trained in the advertising and business fields to shoulder the mission—HERBERT W. ARMSTRONG [p. 26].

How does the Worldwide Church of God view all other churches? "There is ONLY ONE WORK that is preaching the true gospel. . . . THIS IS THAT WORK. Every other work *rejects* the message of Jesus Christ—rejects His RULE through His LAWS. There is no exception!" (*The Plain Truth,* July, 1965, p. 30).

From small beginnings in 1934, the Worldwide Church of God has emerged as a potent religious force. Its present congregation has been estimated to be about 100,000 and its annual income 70 million dollars (*L. A. Times,* Jan. 21, 1979). The Church's magazine, *The Plain Truth,* peaked at 3.8 million copies a month at the end of 1975 and then declined to about 2 million.

The 1970's brought a number of problems to the Armstrong Empire. "Confidence in the Armstrong cause was eroding quite rapidly by the beginning of 1970 as a credibility gap continued to widen regarding his 1972 prophecies" (Marion McNair, *Armstrongism: Religion or Rip-Off?,* p. 203). The years 1972 through 1974 were also critical with dozens of ministers and thousands of members leaving or being disfellowshipped (Joseph Hopkins, *Christianity Today,* Apr. 1, 1977, p. 21). The *L. A. Times* published a number of articles dealing with the difficulties the Church was experiencing, with such headlines as: "Founder of Church Fights Defections," "Garner Ted Show to End," "Father Banishes Garner Ted Armstrong," "State Files Suit Against Armstrong's Empire," and "Receiver Takes Over Armstrong Empire."

While other splits from the Worldwide Church of God had occurred during the decade, the most significant one was brought about by the June 1978 excommunication of Garner Ted, heir apparent to the Armstrong Empire. The following month Ted announced that he had formed his own church, The Church of God, International, in Tyler, Texas, and that he would resume his religious broadcasting. Beginning with one station in San Antonio, by the end of 1979 about 50 were carrying his programs. Several television specials were being shown and new ones were being produced.

Growth of this new church is also evidenced by a 25,000 dollar a week budget, the thousands of incoming letters received each month, the printing of new literature, and the publications *Internews* and *Twentieth Century Watch.* The number of "congregations" is approaching 100 in the U. S., Canada, Australia, England and France. Approximately

2,200 attended the Feast of Tabernacles at one of three sites in 1979 (*Internews,* Nov.-Dec., 1979).

Doctrinally, "Armstrong said his new church will generally follow the doctrines of his father's church" (*L. A. Times,* July 30, 1978, Part 1, p. 3). In the November 21, 1979 issue of *NOW,* Garner Ted wrote to his readers, "I am amazed at the vicious rumors that have been started against us. Some have said we have abandoned the Sabbath and Holy Days and that we are 'watering down' doctrine. That just has not happened."

Appeal

How might the substantial growth of the Worldwide Church of God be explained? What attracts the converts? Salem Kirban well expresses one's typical reactions after a visit to Ambassador College.

> From an earthly standpoint, it appears to be the closest thing to Utopia that I have ever seen!
>
> Humanly speaking, if I were not a Christian, I would quickly join the Armstrong Radio Church of God and attend his college. For it has everything this world has to offer.
>
> And everything Herbert W. Armstrong does is TOP QUALITY! His methods of planning and promotion are without equal! And he is getting results [*The Plain Truth About the Plain Truth,* p. 4].

Joseph Hopkins introduces the subject of the cult's appeal and then lists a number of factors:

> What accounts for the tremendous appeal of the Armstrong movement? The dynamic broadcasts? The slick publications? The use of shock and sensationalism? Skillful use of Madison Avenue's most ingenious devices? There are other factors [*Christianity Today,* Feb. 17, 1971, p. 7].

These may be summarized as: 1) An *image* of committed and

unyielding orthodoxy. 2) Condemnation of what many people "feel are the warning signs of the demise of civilization." 3) ". . . Armstrong has vigorously affirmed the old-fashioned Christian and American virtues of honor, reverence, patriotism, thrift, integrity, chastity, and temperance." 4) In a period of pessimism Armstrong "promises a bright, new, beautiful 'World Tomorrow,' from which all the evils of contemporary society will be eradicated. . . ." He has emphasized the signs of the end times. 5) "In an era of incessant financial appeals . . . it is refreshing to find an operation that appears to be completely non-mercenary. All literature is offered free of charge." There is no pressure to financially contribute or to join (ibid., pp. 7, 8).

Certainly all of the foregoing have contributed to the appeal of the group and its phenomenal growth of 30 percent each year for the first 35 years of its existence (*This is The Worldwide Church of God,* p. 15).

Prophetic Failure

In his book *Armstrongism: Religion or Rip-Off?,* former staff member Marion McNair devotes two entire chapters to discussing and documenting the false predictions of Herbert W. Armstrong and other Church writers. He lists twenty-one major failures in prophecies made between 1938 and mid-1945 (pp. 169, 170), and forty for the years 1947–1972 (pp. 209, 210). In spite of this disasterous record Garner Ted claimed that "major events now taking place in the world were being predicted 35 years ago in *The Plain Truth*" (June 1976, p. 22). A review of some of the predictions made in 1940 and 1941 reveals prophetic failure, not success. It was predicted that: Armageddon was only 3-4 years away, Britain would be invaded and conquered, the U.S. and Britain would "annihilate the Turks from off the earth," America would be conquered and her people transplanted to other lands, the Italians would capture Egypt and Palestine, and Hitler would be the victor in the invasion of Russia (McNair, pp. 165, 166; *Ambassador Report*, p. 53). The events of history have clearly demonstrated that Herbert W. Armstrong and writers of his movement have failed the prophetic test recorded in Deuteronomy 18:20-22.

Doctrines

It is difficult for the researcher to establish the overall teachings of the Worldwide Church of God because they have not been compiled. Rather they are scattered throughout the materials of the group. Thus the potential convert is drawn into the cult with small doses of its distinctive teachings over a period of time.

A presentation of the doctrines of the group may be given in at least two different ways: as they reflect the influence or teachings of other religious groups, or as they are categorized under the major areas of theology. The first approach will be employed here.

The influence of other religious groups. The summary which follows is quoted from the Synopsis of Prof. Paul Benware's doctoral dissertation listed in the bibliography.

Herbert Armstrong strongly denies any indebtedness to the religious concepts, ideas or interpretations of other men. He claims that new truth, embedded in the Bible, has been revealed to him. However, it is the conviction of all outside the Worldwide Church of God, who have studied its system, that it is eclectic. Religious systems which were in existence before the Worldwide Church of God came on the religious scene have had some of their teachings incorporated into Armstrongism.

- *Seventh-day Adventism*
  The influence of Seventh-day Adventism through the Church of God [Stanberry, Missouri]—an offshoot of

Adventism—is readily apparent. Their positions on the place and importance of the Sabbath, the keeping of the Law, the nature and destiny of man and the new birth are nearly identical. Other parallels can be observed in teachings on the human nature of Christ, the atonement of Christ, the definition of sin, individual eschatology and the abstinence from certain foods.

- *The Jehovah's Witnesses*
  Charles T. Russell, founder of this group, lived and wrote long before the theology of the Worldwide Church of God was formulated. Both groups believe that the Trinity is a pagan concept, the Holy Spirit is merely a force, the resurrection body is spiritual, the wicked are annihilated and there is an opportunity for salvation after death.

- *Mormonism*
  There are some strikingly similar teachings with those of the Mormon Church. Especially noteworthy are the teachings that deity is the ultimate goal of man and that God planned the fall of man.

- *British-Israelism*
  British-Israelism is a theory which can be incorporated into a variety of religious systems. It essentially teaches that the so-called ten "lost" tribes of Israel have surfaced in this modern era as the British Commonwealth and the United States of America. Armstrong's British-Israelite theory is identical in detail after detail with the old Anglo-Israel theory which was promoted vigorously by a number of authors around the turn of the century.

- *The Church of God* (Stanberry, Missouri)
  Herbert W. Armstrong severed his relationship with this group but evidently brought several of its unique teachings along with him. Common to both are such teachings as the importance of the name "Church of God," the view of a Wednesday crucifixion with a Saturday resurrection, and

severe condemnation of most holidays as products of paganism.

In a visit to its Pasadena Headquarters in 1976, Dr. Joseph Hopkins asked a Church representative about recent doctrinal changes. These are outlined to Hopkins by Robert Kuhn and reported by Hopkins in "Armstrong's Church of God: Mellowed Aberrations?" (*Christianity Today,* Apr. 15, 1977, pp. 22-24).

What the investigator concludes after a study of the doctrines of the Worldwide Church of God is that most certainly are *not new,* except for their combination being found in one system. An examination and refutation of all of Armstrong's doctrinal deviations would require a large volume. The reader is referred to the Bibliography for sources which further examine and expose his teachings.

Armstrong and the new birth. In *Just What Do You Mean—Born Again?* Armstrong teaches that one who accepts Christ as Savior has not yet been "born again":

- The experience of conversion, in this life, is a begettal—a "conception"—an "impregnation"—but NOT YET A BIRTH! [p. 8].
- That tremendous, glorious event of being BORN of God is to take place AT THE RESURRECTION OF THE JUST—at the time of Christ's second coming to earth! [p. 13].

Scripture is clear that the new birth is accomplished when one believes in Jesus Christ and has nothing to do with the resurrection. The Apostle Peter refutes Armstrong's teaching:

Being born again [past tense, not future. "You have been born again," NASB], not of corruptible seed, but of incorruptible, by the word of God, which liveth and abideth for ever [I Pet. 1:23].

50

The writers of the New Testament view the new birth as synonymous with regeneration to eternal life and those regenerated are viewed as "saved." John the Baptist said, "He that believeth on the Son hath everlasting life . . ." (John 3:36). Jesus said: ". . . He that heareth my word, and believeth on him that sent me, hath everlasting life . . ." (John 5:24). ". . . He that believeth on me hath everlasting life" (John 6:47). The Apostle Paul wrote: "Not by works of righteousness which we have done, but according to his mercy he saved us . . ." (Titus 3:5).

The present writer and all other "born again" Christians accept the Bible's plain truth rather than the "plain truth" of the Worldwide Church of God.

Walter Martin suggests that

> there is one sure remedy to the problem of the spread of Mr. Armstrong's radio religion. Turn off the set and open your Bible, for within its pages God is always broadcasting the eternal message of the Gospel of Grace impregnated by the Spirit of God in every essential necessary to the redemption of the soul and recreation and living of the Christian life [*Herbert W. Armstrong and the Radio Church of God,* p. 32].

BIBLIOGRAPHY

Benware, Paul N. *Ambassadors of Armstrongism: An Analysis of the History and Teachings of the Worldwide Church of God.* Philadelphia: Presbyterian and Reformed Publishing Co., 1975.

Campbell, Roger F. *Herbert W. Armstrong and His Worldwide Church of God: A Critical Examination.* Fort Washington: Christian Literature Crusade, 1974. 120 pp.

DeLoach, Charles F. *The Armstrong Error.* Plainfield, New Jersey: Logos International, 1971. 117 pp. Written by a former member.

Grant, Robert G. *The Plain Truth About the Armstrong Cult.* No imprint. 51 pp.

Hinson, William B. *The Broadway to Armageddon*. Nashville: Religion in the News, 1977. 234 pp. Written by a former WCG minister.

Hopkins, Joseph. *The Armstrong Empire: A Look at the Worldwide Church of God*. Grand Rapids: Wm. B. Eerdmans Publishing Co., 1974. 304 pp. The best treatment on the subject.

Kirban, Salem. *The Plain Truth About the Plain Truth*. Huntington Valley, Pa.: Salem Kirban Inc., 1970. 53pp.

Lowe, Harry W. *Radio Church of God: How Its Teachings Differ From Those of Seventh-day Adventists*. Mountain View, Calif.: Pacific Press Publishing Association, 1970. 143 pp. Lowe is an Adventist.

Marson, Richard A. *The Marson Report Concerning Herbert W. Armstrong*. Seattle, Wash.: The Ashley-Calvin Press, 1970. 175 pp. Written by a former member.

Martin, Walter R. *Herbert W. Armstrong and the Radio Church of God in the Light of the Bible*. Minneapolis: Bethany Fellowship, Inc., Publishers, 1968. 32 pp.

McNair, Marion. *Armstrongism: Religion or Rip-Off? An Exposé of the Armstrong Modus Operandi*. Orlando: Pacific Charters, 1977. 339 pp. The most revealing of books by former members.

Sumner, Robert L. *Armstrongism: The "Worldwide Church of God" Examined in the Searching Light of Scripture*. Brownsburg, Ind.: Biblical Evangelism Press, 1974. 424 pp.

Magazine Articles

Ambassador Review (June 1976) and *Ambassador Report* (1977, Mar.-Apr. 1978—P. O. Box 4068, Pasadena, Calif. 91106). Written and published by former members of the WCG. Devastating exposé of the WCG. Updates of the *Ambassador Report* appear from time to time.

Campbell, Roger. "Herbert W. Armstrong: Does He Really Have the 'Plain Truth'?" *Moody Monthly*, Oct., 1972, pp. 36, 37, 54, 55.

Campbell, Roger. "Herbert W. Armstrong: Mr. Confusion," *The King's Business*, Feb., 1962, pp. 24-27. Reprinted in several forms.

Darby, Knuteson and Campbell. *The Delusions of Herbert W. Armstrong*. A reprint of three articles which appeared in *The Discerner* quarterly of the Religion Analysis Service, Jan.-Mar., 1962 issue.

Hopkins, Joseph Martin. (No Title) *Christianity Today*, Feb. 17, 1971, pp. 6-9.

―――. "Mr. Jones, Meet Herbert W. Armstrong," *Eternity*, Oct., 1972, pp. 19-22, 24, 43.

―――. "Armstrong's Worldwide Church of God: Musical Chairs of Change," *Christianity Today*, Apr. 1, 1977, pp. 20-23; "Armstrong's Church of God: Mellowed Aberrations?" Apr. 15, 1977, pp. 22-24.

Tarr, Leslie. "Herbert W. Armstrong: Does He Really Have the 'Plain Truth'?" *Moody Monthly*, Sept., 1972, pp. 24-27.

Unpublished Materials

Benware, Paul N. "An Analysis of the History and Teachings of the Worldwide Church of God." Unpublished Doctor's Thesis, Grace Theological Seminary, Winona Lake, Indiana, 1973. ("Synopsis").

7

Spiritualism (Spiritism)

The notoriety over the late Bishop James Pike's best seller, *The Other Side* (1968), and his September 3, 1967 televised séance with Arthur Ford, did much to bring Spiritualism back into prominence for the first time in about fifty years. The beginnings of the movement are lost in antiquity, but the rise of Modern Spiritualism dates from March 31, 1848 in the psychic experiences of Margaret and Kate Fox in Hydesville, New York (B. F. Austin, *The A.B.C. of Spiritualism*, Q.3). Some Spiritualists place the modern beginning three years earlier with the spirit-controlled writings of Andrew Jackson Davis. The movement reached its zenith in the United States during the 1850's when it was estimated that there were 1.5 million Spiritualists.

There is disagreement among Christians as to how a study on the subject should be titled: some prefer the term "Spiritualism" and others "Spiritism." Spiritualism is the commonly accepted title used by its adherents and 'Spiritism' is a kind of nickname given to the Spiritualist Movement by its opponents" (J. Stafford Wright, *Man in the Process of Time*, p. 101).

It is a mistake to view Spiritualism as primarily a psychic phenomenon. It is that, but it is also a religion.

Spiritualism is the science that investigates, analyzes, and classifies, all things dealing with Spirit in its various manifestations. It constitutes a true religion when one lives in accordance with its teachings [Edwin B. Morse, *The "Why's" of Spiritualism*, p. 9].

In the following survey several important matters are investigated. What is Spiritualism's appeal? What manifestations are attributed to it? How might these be explained? What do Spiritualists teach? What do Christians who were formerly mediums say about Spiritualism? What does the Bible say about it? The concluding bibliography lists works already cited and materials for further study.

The Appeal of Spiritualism

The reasons for Spiritualism's appeal are not difficult to ascertain. The question, "What lies beyond death?" draws many. The desire to "keep in touch" with the departed attracts others. Some are lured by curiosity. Spiritualism claims to give concrete proof of life after death and enlightenment. This is illustrated in an excerpt from *The National Spiritualist:*

All religious groups are largely theoretical, with respect to theology and practice with the exception of Spiritualism which does not theorize, but which has a direct contact with the teachers and loved ones in the greater life. Spiritualism does not promise a sometime uncertain future in another life after death, it teaches and gives the student experience of spiritual life here and now. Such direct contact and full realization is bliss beyond compare. There are no ceremonies in the Spiritualist church which are not understood by all who participate, no mysteries of theology, all that is required is that the Spiritualist shall be earnest in his desire for more light and more understanding of the beauty of contact with universal truth.

. . . Therefore since life is a school, why waste time any longer in a theatrical kindergarten? Graduate to the understanding of Spiritualism which is the science, philosophy and religion of enlightenment [March, 1961, p. 16].

The Manifestations and Interpretations of Spiritualism

Spiritualism, with its inevitable séances, claims a number of manifestations which are usually classified as of two types: physical and mental. Some examples of the *physical* phenomena are: table tipping, slate writing, rappings, materialization, levitation and Ouija board operation. Examples of *mental* phenomena include: automatic writing, clairvoyance and trance speaking. Many additional examples of each category could be listed.

How are the phenomena to be explained? Spiritualists argue that the genuine manifestations (not fraudulent or merely psychic force) are proof of contact with departed spirits.

The Christian interpretation sees the phenomena as explainable in three possible ways: 1) trickery, 2) psychic force, and 3) demonic activity. Which of the three explanations applies in the individual case is not always easy to determine. It is proven that some Spiritualists have employed trickery. That psychic force can be operative has also been demonstrated (*Man in the Process of Time,* pp. 109, 110) and Spiritualists admit that sometimes the messages received reflect the mind of the sitter (*The A.B.C. of Spiritualism,* Q. 45). They even admit that the "Spirit world contains evil spirits" and "untruthful and deceiving spirits" and that advice received has at times led to tragic results (ibid., Q's. 28, 34, 43). Christianity teaches that the spirits contacted are not those of the dead, but rather fallen angels (demons) who impersonate the dead to deceive and to possess those who call upon them. (For a discussion see Unger's *Demons in the World Today.*) This is why the Bible universally condemns Spiritualism.

The Teachings of Spiritualism

F. E. Mayer accurately stated that "as a religious system spiritualism must be characterized as a complete denial of every Christian truth . . ." (*The Religious Bodies of America,* 4th ed., p. 565). The questions and answers below are all taken from *The A.B.C. of Spiritualism,* a booklet distributed by the National Spiritualist Association of Churches.

● *Is not Spiritualism based upon the Bible?* (Q. 11)
No. The Bible so far as it is inspired and true is based upon Mediumship and therefore, both Christianity . . . and Spiritualism rest on the same basis.

Spiritualism does not depend for its credentials and proofs upon any former revelation.

● *Do Spiritualists believe in the divinity of Jesus?* (Q. 16)
Most assuredly. They believe in the divinity of all men. Every man is divine in that he is a child of God, and inherits a spiritual (divine) nature. . . .

● *Does Spiritualism recognize Jesus as one person of the Trinity, co-equal with the Father, and divine in a sense which divinity is unattainable by other men?* (Q. 17)
No. Spiritualism accepts him as one of many Saviour Christs, who at different times have come into the world to lighten its darkness and show by precept and example the way of life to men. It recognizes him as a world Saviour but not as "the only name" given under heaven by which men can be saved.

● *Does not spiritualism recognize special value and efficacy in the death of Jesus in saving men?* (Q. 19)
No. Spiritualism sees in the death of Jesus an illustration of the martyr spirit, of that unselfish and heroic devotion to humanity which ever characterized the life of Jesus, but no special atoning value in his sufferings and death. . . .

● *From the standpoint of Spiritualism how is the character and work of Jesus to be interpreted?* (Q. 21)

Jesus was a great Mediator, or Medium, who recognized all the fundamental principles of Spiritualism and practiced them. . . .

●*Does Spiritualism recognize rewards and punishments in the life after death?* (Q. 86)

. . . No man escapes punishment, no man misses due reward. The idea of an atoning sacrifice for sins which will remove their natural consequences (pardon) is simply ludicrous to the inhabitants of the spirit spheres.

● *Do the departed, according to Spiritualism, find heaven and hell as depicted by Church teaching?* (Q. 88)

Not at all. . . . They deny any vision of a great white throne, any manifestations of a personal God, any appearance of Jesus, or any lake of fire and torment for lost souls. . . .

Additional denials of biblical doctrine could be quoted, but it is obvious that Spiritualism represents a system which rejects orthodox Christianity.

Two Former Spiritualists

Raphael Gasson and Victor Ernest were mediums before they became Christians. Both have written books giving their experiences.

In *The Challenging Counterfeit,* Gasson wrote:

The journey, for me, from Satan to Christ, was a long and weary one, taking dangerous pathways, bringing many bitter experiences and battles against principalities and powers, almost costing my life, before I reached that place called Calvary—where the Lord Jesus Christ met my need as a sinner as I surrendered my life to Him [p. 1].

. . . We find that Spiritualism is one of the most fiendish of Satan's methods of instilling lying deceptions into the minds of people. Having tested the spirits and the claims they make through their mediums, we most certainly find them contrary to the Word of God, which tells us most explicitly that "in the latter times, some shall depart from the faith, giving heed to seducing spirits, and doctrines of devils'' (I Tim. 4:1) [p. 92].

In *I Talked with Spirits,* Victor Ernest explains how demonic interference continued years after his conversion.

> Sometimes my memory would go blank; other times my throat would constrict and I couldn't speak. As soon as I prayed for help through the power of Jesus' blood, the attack ceased and I continued. These assaults continued sporadically for thirteen years before my spiritual defenses were built up to keep demons from penetrating my body [p. 59].

In a question-and-answer séance shortly before his conversion Rev. Ernest relates the following:

> When the trumpet returned for my third and last question, I reviewed what the spirit had said. "O spirit, you believe that Jesus is the son of God, that he is the Savior of the world—do you believe that Jesus died on the cross and shed his blood for the remission of sin?"

> The medium, deep in a trance, was catapulted off his chair. He fell in the middle of the living room floor and lay groaning as if in deep pain. The turbulent sounds suggested spirits in a carnival of confusion [p. 32].

These quotations reveal the source and dangers of Spiritualism and the deliverance to be found in Christ.

The Bible on Spiritualism

Spiritualists often argue as though Spiritualism were the true successor of Christianity as set forth in the New Testament.

> How—it may be asked—should Christianity be opposed to Spiritualism when the Christian Religion was really born in a Seance? The real beginning of Christianity, its motive power, its great impetus, came—not from the birth or death of Jesus—but from Pentecost, the greatest Seance in history [*The A.B.C. of Spiritualism,* Q. 23].

They do admit that there are "a few isolated passages" in the Old Testament which forbid "the practice of communicating with spirits" (ibid:, Q. 22). This statement fails to recognize the fact that in Israel necromancy (consulting the dead) was "viewed as flagrant apostasy from Jehovah and as a crime punishable by the severest penalties" (Merrill F. Unger, *Biblical Demonology*, p. 144).

- Regard not them that have familiar spirits, neither seek after wizards, to be defiled by them: I *am* the Lord your God [Lev. 19:31].
- And the soul that turneth after such as have familiar spirits, and after wizards, to go a whoring after them, I will even set my face against that soul, and will cut him off from among his people [Lev. 20:6].
- A man also or woman that hath a familiar spirit, or that is a wizard, shall surely be put to death: they shall stone them with stones: their blood *shall be* upon them [Lev. 20:27].
- There shall not be found among you . . . that useth divination, *or* an observer of times, or an enchanter, or a witch, or a charmer, or a consulter with familiar spirits, or a wizard, or a necromancer [Deut. 18:10, 11].
- [Manasseh] . . . dealt with familiar spirits and wizards: he wrought much wickedness in the sight of the Lord, to provoke *him* to anger [II Kings 21:6].
- Moreover the *workers with* familiar spirits, and the wizards, . . . did Josiah put away, that he might perform the words of the law which were written in the book that Hilkiah the priest found in the house of the Lord [II Kings 23:24].
- So Saul died for his transgression which he committed against the Lord, *even* against the word of the Lord, which he kept not, and also for asking *counsel of one that had* a familiar spirit, to enquire *of it;* and enquired not of the Lord: therefore he slew him, and turned the kingdom unto David the son of Jesse [I Chron. 10:13, 14].
- And when they shall say unto you, Seek unto them that have familiar spirits, and unto wizards that peep, and that mutter: should not a people seek unto their

God? . . . To the law and to the testimony: if they speak not according to this word, *it is* because *there is* no light in them [Isa. 8:19, 20].

After an examination of these and other passages, J. Stafford Wright concluded:

Whatever may be the precise rendering of any single passage, it is beyond doubt that the Old Testament bans any attempt to contact the departed. This is true of the law, the historical books, and the prophets. Is there the slightest sign that the New Testament lifts the ban? [*Christianity and the Occult,* p. 112].

Conclusion

Spiritualism must be rejected not only because what it teaches is anti-biblical, but also because of the harm it can bring to those who devote themselves to it. As Raphael Gasson warned, *"The way into Spiritualism is extraordinarily easy, the way out is extremely dangerous"* (*The Challenging Counterfeit,* p. 19).

BIBLIOGRAPHY

Ernest, Victor H. *I Talked with Spirits*. Wheaton: Tyndale House Publishers, 1970.

Gasson, Raphael. *The Challenging Counterfeit*. Plainfield, New Jersey: Logos International, 1966.

Martin, Walter R. *The Kingdom of the Cults*. Rev. ed.; Minneapolis: Bethany Fellowship, 1965. Spiritualism treated, pp. 199-212.

Mayer, F. E. *The Religious Bodies of America*. 4th ed.; St. Louis, Mo.: Concordia Publishing House, 1961. Spiritualism treated, pp. 563-567.

Pember, G. H. *Earth's Earliest Ages*. Old Tappan, New Jersey: Fleming H. Revell Company, n.d. Spiritualism treated, pp. 243-391.

Unger, Merrill F. *Biblical Demonology*. Wheaton: Scripture Press, 1952.

————. *Demons in the World Today*. Wheaton: Tyndale House Publishers, 1971.

————. *The Haunting of Bishop Pike: A Christian View of the Other Side*. Wheaton: Tyndale House Publishers, 1971.

Van Baalen, J. K. *The Chaos of the Cults*. 4th rev. ed.; Wm. B. Eerdmans Publishing Co., 1962. Spiritualism treated, pp. 31-61. The case of the witch (medium) of Endor is taken up on pp. 51-54.

Wright, J. Stafford. *Christianity and the Occult*. Chicago: Moody Press, 1971.

————. *Man in the Process of Time*. Grand Rapids: Wm. B. Eerdmans Publishing Co., 1956.

Spiritualist Materials

The A.B.C. of Spiritualism, The "Why's" of Spiritualism and *The National Spiritualist* magazine are all published by the National Spiritualist Association of Churches, 11811 Watertown Plank Road, Milwaukee, Wisconsin.

8

Seventh-day Adventism

Of the many groups which have been classified as "cults," the Seventh-day Adventist Church is one of the most puzzling for the researcher. Evaluations of this group range from strong condemnation, to approval with reservations. Some of the strongest voices against recognition of Adventism as an evangelical body have been former adherents (D. M. Canright, E. B. Jones and R. A. Greive). In 1956, acceptance of the Adventists as evangelical (while recognizing some doctrinal errors) came from Walter R. Martin, E. Schuyler English (*Our Hope*, November, 1956) and Donald Grey Barnhouse (*Eternity*, September, 1956). Walter Martin presented the full account of his findings and conclusions in *The Truth About Seventh-day Adventism* (1960). While not an answer to Martin's treatment, Norman F. Douty's *Another Look at Seventh-day Adventism* (1962) should be read if one wants the other side of the issue. Douty concluded that as

> long as Adventism denies, explicitly or implicitly, doctrines which the church of Christ as a whole has always declared; and declares, explicitly or implicitly, doctrines which the church of Christ as a whole has always denied, it cannot be esteemed a Scriptural church [p. 188].

It is clear that the Adventist leadership wishes recognition as an evangelical body, but the distinctive doctrines of this group have perpetuated its isolation among evangelicals. In 1957 the Review and Herald Publishing Association published *Seventh-day Adventists Answer Questions on Doctrine* which was written by "a Representative Group of Seventh-day Adventist leaders, Bible Teachers and Editors" (title page). The writers of this book explain that the aim

> was to set forth our basic beliefs in terminology currently used in theological circles. This was *not* to be a new statement of faith, but rather an answer to specific questions concerning our faith [p. 8].

This volume was the first *comprehensive* statement of the Seventh-day Adventist "denomination in the area of church doctrine and prophetic interpretation" (p. 8). The book was obviously an effort to give the Adventist answer to the question whether it should be viewed as a sect or an evangelical body. Many reviewers of this book concluded with John H. Gerstner that they were "still unconvinced of Seventh-day Adventism's adequate credal orthodoxy" (*The Theology of the Major Sects,* p. 10).

There is much within the Seventh-day Adventist Church that is praiseworthy: its emphasis on public health and medical missions; its recognition of the sanctity of the home and marriage; its separation from worldliness; its educational and publishing programs; and its adherence to many orthodox doctrines. Undoubtedly, many Adventists are truly regenerate people.

Adventist growth and outreach have been substantial during the 1970's. In 1977 over 240,000 new members were added to the church and membership was 3.2 million in 1979 (566,000 in North America). Work was being done in 100 languages in 192 countries (*Christianity Today,* February 8, 1980, p. 64). Statistics on Adventist medical, welfare, radio ("Voice of Prophecy"), educational and publishing activities are equally impressive.

In the survey which follows there is a brief presentation of the origin of the Seventh-day Adventist denomination. The inside testimony of Rev. R. A. Greive helps to place this church in clearer perspective. An annotated bibliography concludes the study.

History

The Seventh-day Adventist Church arose out of the great second advent awakening which appeared in the early decades of the nineteenth century and which swept through America and many parts of South America, Africa and Asia. In America, William Miller (1782-1849) led the movement. After his conversion he joined the Baptist church in 1816 and later became a licensed minister. Miller took an interest in prophetic themes and after two years of diligent study he concluded that Christ's return would occur in 1843. He lectured widely and "Adventist congregations were raised up in more than a thousand places, numbering some fifty thousand believers" (*Your Friends the Adventists*, p. 85).

The date set for the Lord's return, March 21, 1843, did not come to fulfillment and after recalculation it was concluded that the figures were wrong by a year. When this date also failed, another way of reckoning time was followed and October 22, 1844 was then set. The failure of this date caused the majority of Miller's followers to leave the movement. Miller admitted his mistake and did not accept any of the new theories originated after "The Great Disappointment." He never became a Seventh-day Adventist (*The Truth About Seventh-day Adventism*, pp. 29-30). Seventh-day Adventism began with the conclusion of Hiram Edson (received in a vision) that October 22, 1844 was correct, but that they had been wrong about what would take place on that date. This reinterpretation produced the Adventists' doctrines of the heavenly sanctuary and investigative judgment.

Of the Millerites who did not drop out of the movement, three groups emerged with distinctive doctrines which later fused into the Seventh-day Adventist Church:

> the group headed by Hiram Edson in western New York State which emphasized the doctrine of the heavenly sanctuary; the group in Washington, New Hampshire, which along with Joseph Bates, advocated the observance of the seventh day; and the group around Portland, Maine, which held that Ellen G. White was a true prophetess, whose visions and words were to be followed by Adventists [Anthony A. Hoekema, *The Four Major Cults*, p. 98].

It was Ellen G. White (1827-1915) who played the leading role in the history and doctrinal formation of the movement. "Almost every aspect of belief and activity of the Seventh-day Adventists was encouraged or inspired by a vision or word from Mrs. White" (*The Four Major Cults*, p. 97). (The details of the history of the SDA are found in the books by Damsteegt, Froom, Hoekema and Martin—all are listed in the bibliography.)

By 1855 the three groups merged and headquarters were established at Battle Creek, Michigan. In 1860 the name "Seventh-day Adventist" was officially adopted and in 1863 the General Conference, the top echelon of the Church, was organized. The headquarters were moved to Takoma Park, Washington, D. C. in 1903.

How Should the SDA Church Be Viewed?

(the Testimony of R. A. Greive)

Lengthy articles and books have been written discussing whether or not the Seventh-day Adventist Church should be considered evangelical. The testimony by Pastor R. A. Greive, "Why I was Excommunicated from the SDA Church" (Reprinted by permission from *The King's Business*, July, 1958, pp. 18, 19) does help one to understand why many find it difficult to accept the Adventists as evangelical. Mr. Greive certainly did not write as an uninformed outsider or a novice on the subject. The article gives the information that he "was a Seventh-day Adventist pastor for 30 years and the former president of the North New Zealand Conference of the Seventh-day Adventist Church." The account is also valuable because it was written after the SDA were declared to be an evangelical group.

"[Several] years ago certain American editors reported that the Seventh-day Adventist church had reworked its theology to the point that the SDA movement should now be considered evangelical.

"At the very moment these Christian editors in America were extending the right hand of fellowship to the leaders of Adventism, I and three other SDA ministers were being tried for heresy in Australia. What I saw at that trial convinced me how hopelessly mistaken were these American editors.

"It all began when we four ministers came with hungry, seeking hearts to the New Testament revelation of the Gospel. We made the great discovery of the doctrine of justification and found its dynamics too much to contain in earthen vessels. We literally spilled over with the good news. Many in our congregations came to believe in Biblical justification and many of us hailed it as the dawn of a new day for Adventism. But its triumph was short-lived.

"We ministers were placed on trial and when we failed to recant were summarily dismissed from the SDA ministry. But we did not go alone. Spiritually-enlightened members numbering more than 100 resigned from their SDA churches seeking to find fellowship and happiness within various branches of God's earthly church. This was not a mass movement from one Adventist church but an intelligent separation on the part of schoolteachers, businessmen and other thinking people from many places in Australia and New Zealand.

"They moved out because they were convinced that the basic doctrines and prophetical interpretations of their church were at variance with the revelation of Scripture.

"Our crime consisted in sharing the good news that God in Christ had completely forgiven us our sins, so blotting out the record of wrong doing that the judgment and condemnation resulting therefrom was entirely lifted and the believer restored to sonship and heirship with Christ. These New Testament concepts conflicted with the published statements of Ellen G. White who had declared, 'It is impossible that the sins of men should be blotted out until after the judgment (commencing in 1844) at which their cases are to be investigated' (*Great Controversy*, p. 485). Hence we were indicted for believing that the Bible alone was the sole source of faith and doctrine and was its own interpreter as against the overriding authority of the writings of Ellen G. White.

"The point of issue was whether a Seventh-day Adventist minister could lay aside the authority of Mrs. White's writings in favor of the Bible and still be a minister of the SDA church. The answer at our trail was an unequivocal *no*.

"These heresy trials were to us ordeals by fire. There was all the evidence of carefully-planned psychological warfare. There was also the make-believe of prayer and investigation of the themes of salvation as presented. But back and behind everything was the resolve on the part of the 13 men on the committee to force a surrender to the E. G. White interpretations, no matter what evidence there was to the contrary.

"When the committee failed to break down a defendant a private session with the chairman and his secretary was held. At this private session all subtleties were cast aside. And when we failed to recant we were excommunicated and ruined over night.

"We who were once the ardent supporters of the SDA church now see that it is not in the Protestant succession. We also know that SDA special doctrines—Sabbath, sanctuary, investigative judgment, remnant church—are unalterable, unchangeable beliefs. To change any one of these doctrines is to compromise the prophetic standing of Mrs. White and that the SDA leaders will never do because it is their firm belief that Mrs. White's prophetic gift is the outstanding mark of their remnant church.

"In theory Adventists exalt the Bible above the writings of Mrs. White. In practice they do exactly the opposite. The psychological power and effects of her writings and interpretations so subtly enslave the minds of ministers and members alike that I doubt if ever they relize that it is *her* revelations they are believing and not those of the Bible. As an illustration of this subtle enslavement, more than 30 years ago as a young minister entering upon his life work, I read the Epistle to the Hebrews in the Greek text and was astonished and mystified that I could not fit my Adventist beliefs of the sanctuary into the teaching of this portion of Scripture. My faith in the writings of Mrs. White were such that unhesitatingly I laid the Bible teaching aside in favor of what my church taught.

"During our trials F. G. Clifford, head of the SDA church here, put it on record as the denominational position that 'the writings of Mrs. White are inspired by the same Spirit that inspired the Bible; therefore we must have the same faith in the writings of Mrs. White as we have in the Bible.' Again, 'This is our denominational position, that God forgives neither absolutely nor finally.'

"Consistent with the SDA demand for implicit faith in Mrs. White is a recent article appearing in the *Australasian Record* titled, 'The Unchanging Unchangeable Truth.' It was written by the head of the Australasian SDA church. Said this learned gentleman: 'No fresh presentation, or clearer outline will ever change or diminish the force of the truth of the foundational doctrines which have made us a distinct people. Unfortunately some of our people have gained the impression that there is developing within the church some change in attitude toward the *Spirit of Prophecy* [writings of Mrs. White] and also toward the nature of the work of Christ in the cleansing of the sanctuary. It is even suggested by some that the General Conference [USA ruling body of SDAs] is considering the matter of presenting a changed viewpoint to our people on these subjects. *We desire to state unequivocably that such statements are not true; they do not bear a semblance of truth.'*

"The writer of this article then quoted W. R. Beach, secretary of the General Conference, who had written to assure the Australasian division of SDAs that their fears of any impending changes in doctrine were altogether groundless. 'We have made it clear here at the seminary and elsewhere,' said Beach, 'that there is no altering of our position, no new pronouncement. . . .'

"The doctrinal and prophetical edifice of Adventism rests not on the Bible alone, but upon Mrs. White and the Bible. This duality of revelation under interpretation of the 'secondary' revelation creates a freak religion that is in no way related to full-blooded Protestantism. When I was on trial the committee essayed to give me 16 quotations from extra-canonical sources to prove that a believer's sins are all upon the record until after the investigative judgment. But in their presentation there was not a single Bible text.

"Adventism and justification cannot live together. At my trial the secretary reasoned thus: 'If Brother Greive is right on justification and no record of a believer's sins remains upon the books, then verily there is no investigative judgment; and if there is no investigative judgment then no Adventist movement of 1844; and if no Adventist movement the whole prophetic interpretation of Daniel 8:13, 14 is gone.'

"But Seventh-day Adventism must not be dismissed as unworthy of notice. It has an attractive side and a driving force worthy of a better cause. Their members are selfless in their devotion and loyal to its creed and to its propagation. There is personal sacrifice in giving and service that is altogether astonishing. The expansion of their movement is phenomenal and their activities worldwide. Their members are honorable and lovable in the main. All this makes the task of their enlightenment one of the greatest facing Christendom today. And they are stuck in the mud of their pharisaical pride that 'we are God's very own people. We have a prophetess that no other modern religion has. We keep the 10 commandments. We pay our tithes and offerings.'

"Indeed the task of winning them will be difficult. As an Adventist minister for 30 years, I know there will be no change from within. True, the cruder form of their doctrines is giving way to a more polished expression of the same. But the hard core of original Adventist doctrine persists. A few minor changes and modifications will never make Adventism a New Testament church in the Protestant succession. It will have to be rebuilt from the bottom up."

(For an updating and examination of the theological developments and controversy in the SDA Church the reader is referred to the article by Edward Plowman and the book *The Shaking of Adventism* listed in the bibliography.)

BIBLIOGRAPHY

Bird, Herbert S. "Adventists," *The Encyclopedia of Christianity*, I, pp. 79-93. Bird concludes: ". . . If a reconciliation between SDA and evangelical Protestantism is to be effected, it will require either that the former so revise its basic principles as practically to cease to be what it is, or that the latter deny the faith" (p. 92).

————. *Theology of Seventh-day Adventism*. Grand Rapids: Wm. B. Eerdmans Publishing Co., 1961. A good analysis of Seventh-day Adventism but criticized by Martin. Chapter 8 deals with "Seventh-day Adventism and Evangelical Faith."

Canright, D. M. *Seventh-day Adventism Refuted*. Nashville: B. C. Goodpasture, 1962. "A reprint of a series of ten tracts copyrighted and published by D. M. Canright in 1889."

————. *Seventh-day Adventism Renounced*. Nashville: Gospel Advocate Co., reprinted 1961. Originally published in 1889, this is a reprint of the 1914, fourteenth edition. The author was an Adventist for 28 years and a prominent SDA minister before he left. He presents reasons why he left the movement and refutes SDA doctrines.

Norman F. Douty defends Canright against the Adventist attacks upon him in his book *The Case of D. M. Canright*. Grand Rapids: Baker Book House, 1964.

Damsteegt, P. Gerard. *Foundations of the Seventh-day Adventist Message and Mission*. Grand Rapids: Wm. B. Eerdmans Publishing Co., 1977. A well-documented, comprehensive and careful study by a SDA which traces the development of Adventist (Millerite) and SDA ideas and theology from the beginning of the 19th century to the year 1874. The author explains that the study attempts to present an "understanding of the origins and basic structure of the theology which has motivated the Seventh-day Adventist Church for more than a century . . .(xiii).

DeHaan, M. R. "What do Seventh-day Adventists Believe Today?" *The King's Business,* October, 1959, pp. 28-33.

DeHaan, Richard W. "Who Changed the Sabbath?" Grand Rapids: The Radio Bible Class, 1967. An answer to the SDAs on the subject.

Douty, Norman F. *Another Look at Seventh-day Adventism*. Grand Rapids: Baker Book House, 1962. A careful study based upon *Questions on Doctrine* and other SDA sources. In the Conclusion, pp. 182-189, Douty finds that Adventism is characterized by features which disqualify it as an evangelical body.

Gerstner, John H. *The Theology of the Major Sects*. Grand Rapids: Baker Book House, 1960. Adventism is treated pp. 19-28.

Hoekema, Anthony A. *The Four Major Cults*. Grand Rapids: Wm. B. Eerdmans Publishing Co., 1963. Adventism is treated pp. 89-169. Argues that Adventism must be regarded as a cult because it manifests the traits distinctive of a cult; "Is Seventh-day Adventism a Cult?," pp. 388-403.

Jewett, Paul K. *The Lord's Day: A Theological Guide to the Christian Day of Worship*. Grand Rapids: Wm. B. Eerdmans publishing Co., 1971 (Fuller Theological Seminary, 1978).

Lewis, Gordon R. *The Bible, the Christian and Seventh-day Adventism (Adventists)*. Philadelphia: Presbyterian and Reformed Publishing Co., 1966. "If Adventism is not ardent evangelicalism or typical cultism then how shall it be classified? The evidence supports Dr. Lindsell's [Dr. Harold Lindsell, Editor, *Christianity Today*] judgment that it is similar to Romanism. Like Romanism, Adventism has added to the Scripture a body of tradition it seems reluctant to break. Like Romanism Adventism depreciates the completeness of Christ's work of atonement, and like Romanism Adventism adds to grace the necessity of human works as a condition of salvation. . . . The error of Romanism and Adventism resembles that of the Galatians . . ." (p. 28).

Martin, Walter R. *The Kingdom of the Cults*. Rev. ed.; Minneapolis: Bethany Fellowship, Inc., 1965. In an appendix (pp. 360-423) he answers those who still find Adventism a cult and defends his position that they are not.

————. *The Truth About Seventh-day Adventism*. Grand Rapids: Zondervan Publishing House, 1960. Martin defends the SDA church as an evangelical body while he is also very critical of a number of distinctive Adventist doctrines.

A former SDA, Mary Lyons, questions whether Martin's book is "Really 'The Truth' " about the SDAs in *The King's Business*, July, 1960, pp. 27-29.

Paxton, Geoffrey J. *The Shaking of Adventism*. Grand Rapids: Baker Book House, 1978. "A documented account of the crisis among Adventists over the doctrine of justification by faith" (front cover).

Plowman, Edward E., "The Shaking of Adventism?"

Christianity Today, Feb. 8, 1980, pp. 64-67. Subtitle: "SDA biblical scholars challenge the traditionalists." In agreement with some other writers on Adventism, Plowman states, "In the last two decades the church has moved closer to the evangelical mainstream" (p. 65).

Talbot, Louis T. "Why Seventh-day Adventism is *Not* Evangelical," *The King's Business,* April-June, 1957. Written in reply to the declaring of the Adventists as evangelical in 1956.

Adventist Sources

Froom, Leroy Edwin. *The Prophetic Faith of our Fathers.* 4 vols. Washington, D.C.: Review and Herald Publishing Association, 1946-54. Volume IV presents the history of the SDA Church.

Maxwell, A. S. *Your Friends the Adventists.* Mountain View, Calif.: Pacific Press Publishing Association, 1967.

Seventh-day Adventists Answer Questions on Doctrine. Washington, D.C.: Review and Herald Publishing Association, 1957. The most recent official statement of SDA doctrine. It deals with questions submitted by Walter Martin. That the book represented the feeling of all SDAs is open to question.

"A. L. Hudson, former elder in a large Adventist Church in Oregon, in company with retired yet powerful Adventist leader Dr. M. L. Andreasen, has spearheaded a move to have those responsible for the publication of *Questions on Doctrine* censured for 'misrepresenting the historic position' of the Adventist church" (*Christianity Today,* Dec. 19, 1960, p. 24). Geoffrey Paxton wrote that "at present there is evidence of a retraction of what was written in *Questions on Doctrine.* I have heard Adventist leaders speak of it as 'damnable heresy.' I have seen letters from Washington, D.C., making it plain that the present leadership of the church is much opposed to the book" (*The Shaking of Adventism,* p. 153).

Additional bibliographies of key Adventist materials will be found in Damsteegt, pp. 313-334; Douty, pp. 209-212; Hoekema, pp. 424-427, and both of Martin's books.

9

"New" Cults and the Occult in the Age of Aquarius

Astrologers tell us that the Age of Aquarius was supposed to bring with it a new religious atmosphere. As John Godwin observed: "It has become difficult to venture anywhere in contemporary America without being informed that the Age of Aquarius is upon us. There's no escaping the message" (*Occult America*, p. 1). Interest in religion, the occult, mysticism and Eastern religion has never been more popular in America. "The last ten years have witnessed a virtual explosion of new religions" (John Weldon, *International Review of Mission*, Oct., 1978, p. 407). Religion is one of the fastest growing fields of graduate study at secular universities today. These facts are striking because during the 1960's some Protestant theologians were erroneously asserting the "death of God" and the soon demise of religion.

In their learned opinion supernaturalism of any sort was no longer a believable option for intelligent people, just as fairy tales are incredible to a rational adult. In fact, those radicals prophesied that religion as a whole seemed slated to disappear, a kind of cultural fog evaporating before the rising sun of scientific knowledge.

But to judge by the course of events in the early 1970's those radicals are going to be exposed as false prophets. Religion, whether traditional Christianity or the latest brand of spiritism, is not dying out by any means; instead, it is experiencing a tremendous upsurge [Vernon C. Grounds, *Christian Heritage,* January, 1973, p. 5].

The significance of this upsurge was recognized and interpreted in a 1972 book by U.S. News and World Report, *The Religious Reawakening in America.*

At a time when established religion has become an object of criticism, we have moved into what many consider to be one of the most religious periods in the history of the United States.

Young people particularly have sparked the revival of interest in spiritual values. Unfulfilled by the offering of the traditional church and the traditional temple, they have slipped into rebellion—not against God and religious values but against the "establishment" of Christian, Jewish, and other faiths. They are searching for new forms and ways of achieving spiritual satisfaction to offset the dulling and sterile effect of a highly materialistic and technological society [p. 11].

The revival of interest in religion and spiritual values led many to accept beliefs and practices which are antithetical to orthodox Christianity (and Judaism). This result was verified by Peter Rowley:

In 1970 about two and a half million people belonged to the new religions of America—Indian, Sino-Japanese, avant-garde Christian and others even more unusual. . . .

Reports indicate that growth in the latter part of 1970 may be as great as a million people seeking an answer to what seems to them a frightening world; young Americans and some middle-aged and older ones all across the U.S. are joining occult religions or following Eastern and Western gurus and abandoning traditional Christianity and Judaism [*New Gods in America,* pp. 3, 4].

What has caused the interest in the occult? What is responsible for the swing toward Eastern religion and mysticism? What are the "new" cults, and which are the most important? These questions are dealt with in the material which follows. A bibliography which includes material cited and for further study concludes the treatment.

The Occult Craze

T. K. Wallace investigated the question, "What's behind the Occultism Craze?" by questioning people in bookstores which specialized in occult material. What were these people seeking?

"I believe there's a master plan to the cosmos, and I want to learn it," said one person. "I need something like horoscopes or Tarot cards to make my decisions for me," said another. "My marriage is on the rocks. I need to find happiness somewhere," a third told me. Still another said, "My life is dull, and I must find something exciting" [*Family Weekly,* Feb. 28, 1971, p. 4].

Many have been influenced to study the occult by the many books on the subject, some of which have been best sellers. It does not require a keen observer to discern the abundance of books on this topic in bookstores, on paperback racks in markets and drug stores, and in public libraries. The occult has been given much exposure in newpapers, magazines and on television. Many public schools and colleges offer courses dealing with witchcraft, astrology and like subjects.

Dr. Krippner contended that the occult revival could be traced to the fact "that many people are having experiences that are not explained by tradition or by education" (ibid.). Occultism seems to promise an answer. Many find the occult a place of "escape from the world's problems and from their own" (ibid.).

Many additional suggestions might be given to explain the

occult craze, but frequently the ultimate cause is ignored or rejected. The present writer agrees with Hal Lindsey's analysis as reported by John Dart in the *Los Angeles Times:*

> Satan changed his strategy about 1967 . . . and has since sought to have the world believe in the supernatural.

> This helps to explain the interest in the occult, witchcraft, Satanism, astrology, Oriental mysticism and similar cults in the last few years [Mar. 10, 1973, p. 25]. An investigation of the occult craze quickly convinces the alert investigator that the interest in this subject and its influence in American life is far more serious than one would like to believe.

The Eastern Influence

What has caused the swing of many Americans, especially young people, to Eastern Religion and mysticism? The answer is not simple, but some valuable suggestions have been given by Oswald Guinness in his article, ''The Eastern Look of the Modern West.'' He sees three basic reasons:

- Western science and philosophy became too mechanistic and rationalistic. They ended up with dry, arid linguistics and a cage-like universe. All this crippled human sensitivity, human imagination and sheer subjective experience. In reaction, many nineteenth-century western people . . . were already turning toward the East. It gave them a basis for imagination and experience when the West was extremely dry and mechanistic.

- . . . In the last 100 years we've seen a resurgence of the whole Eastern culture. . . .

The work of the various eastern apologists is most important of all. . . .

They have traveled widely in the West and have tried to show that where western Christianity has failed and western, post-Christian philosophy has no answers, the East has provided the answers. They have a broad appeal on our campuses. . . .

- The third and most important factor behind the swing to the East is what Alan Watts calls parallelism. I call this dovetailing, the coinciding of post-Christian, western thinking and ancient eastern thinking. The primary cause of dovetailing has not been the direct intellectual influence of the East on the West. Rather, by playing with the options it has, the West has gotten to the place where its only choice is to adhere to what the East has always believed [*His,* Feb., 1972, pp. 2, 3].

Guinness makes another significant observation relative to Eastern religion and orthodox Christianity: "I'm appalled to see how many evangelical Christians accept eastern ideas uncritically without knowing where they came from. Many are completely naive" (ibid., p. 5).

What can the Christian do in the light of this move toward the East? In a day when people are streaming out toward the East, the East is proving to be less than adequate at many points. We need to be among those who call our generation to be realistic, pointing out the errors in the direction they are going. We must show clearly that the East is no exit. And then we must demonstrate the alternative that Christianity offers [*His,* March, 1972, p. 31].

The New Cults

As a teacher of a college course dealing with the "Cults of America" it became obvious during the 1960's that the cult scene was changing and that a number of "new" cults were becoming important. (By "new" it is to be understood that: they were new to America; new as originating in America; or new as reflecting great growth in recent years. The term "cult" is being used in a broad sense.) The usual course in cults included such groups as the Jehovah's Witnesses, Mormons and Christian Scientists. Among the new breed of cults confronting Christianity are: Divine Light Mission, Unification Church, Scientology, Nichiren Shoshu, Bahai, The Church Universal and Triumphant, TM and Hare Krishna.

The older cults were basically a perversion of biblical truth—heresy—holding doctrines which had been rejected by the Church. The new cults are often closely related to the Eastern religions and the occult rather than to Christianity.

In *New Gods in America,* Peter Rowley estimated the following of a number of "The New Religions" in 1970: Scientology (600,000); Nichiren Shoshu (200,000); Spiritual Scientists (Spiritualists, 150,000); Maharishi (Transcendental Meditation), I Ching and Yoga (125,000 each); Black Muslims and Bahai (100,000 each); Association for Research and Enlightenment (13,000); Meher Baba (7,000); Gurdjieff, Witchcraft and Satanic Cults (5,000 each); Zen (2,000); Subud and Hare Krishna (1,500 each) [pp. 3, 4]. It should be remembered that the numbers of followers of these cults must be increased to reflect the growth since 1970 and that these figures do not include the worldwide membership of some of the groups. For example, Nichiren Shoshu (Soka Gakkai) had a following in Japan of "seven million five hundred thousand families . . ." (ibid., p. 177). Scientology with 600,000 adherents in America has a total membership variously estimated as from two to fifteen million. Other examples could be given.

Although Rowley excluded astrology from the list of new religions, millions have substituted it for religion and it has a vital part in many of the new cults. Estimates place 10,000 professional and 175,000 part-time astrologers in America alone, and more than 40 million Americans are said to allow astrology to influence their lives.

Conclusion

What should the Christian's attitude and action be toward adherents of the new cults and the occult in the Age of Aquarius? The Christian must assert the claims of Christ: ". . . I am the way, the truth, and the life: no man cometh unto the Father, but by me" (John 14:6). The search in life for spiritual satisfaction, peace, happiness, fulfillment, excitement, help in decision making and in the problems of life, can all be realized in a personal relationship with Jesus Christ.

Many of the new cults speak of reincarnation— Christianity proclaims the resurrection of Jesus Christ from the dead (I Cor. 15). The man "in Christ" has a satisfying present as well as a sure future (Phil. 4:19; Eph. 1:3-14). Guinness indicated that Eastern religion "is no exit," and the same may be said of the occult. Many religions, gurus and "saviors" have come and gone, but the Lord Jesus Christ is "the same yesterday, and today, and for ever" (Heb. 13:8).

BIBLIOGRAPHY

Books

Enroth, Ronald. *The Lure of the Cults*. Chappaqua, New York: Christian Herald Books, 1979.

————. *Youth Brainwashing and the Extremist Cults*. Grand Rapids: Zondervan Publishing House, 1977.

Godwin, John. *Occult America*. Garden City, New York: Doubleday & Co., Inc., 1972.

Lindsay, Hal, with C. C. Carlson. *Satan is Alive and Well on Planet Earth*. Grand Rapids: Zondervan Publishing House, 1972.

McBeth, Leon. *Strange New Religions*. Nashville: Broadman Press, 1977.

Newman, Joseph (ed.). *The Religious Reawakening in*

America. Washington, D. C.: U. S. News & World Report, Inc., 1972.

Newport, John P. *Christ and the New Consciousness*. Nashville: Broadman Press, 1978.

Petersen, William J. *Those Curious New Cults*. New Canaan, Connecticut: Keats Publishing Co., 1973.

Rowley, Peter. *New Gods in America*. New York: David McKay Co., Inc., 1971.

Sparks, Jack. *The Mind Benders: A Look At Current Cults*. Nashville: Thomas Nelson, Inc., 1977.

Wilburn, Gary. *The Fortune Sellers*. Glendale, California: Regal Books Division, G/L Publications, 1972.

Magazine Articles

Breese, Dave. "The Unholy Spirit of the Age," *Action,* Fall, 1972, pp. 9-13.

Grounds, Vernon C. "Understanding the Neo-mystical Movement," *Christian Heritage,* Jan., 1973, pp. 4-7.

———. "The Revolt Against Rationalism," *Christian Heritage,* Feb., 1973, pp. 26-28, 32.

Guinness, Oswald. "The Eastern Look of the Modern West," *His,* Feb., 1972, pp. 2-5.

———. "The East No Exit," *His,* March, 1972, pp. 27-31.

Petersen, William J. "Contemporary Cults," *Eternity,* Dec., 1971-Sept., 1972. A ten-article series dealing with: "Why Our Kids are into Cults," Astrology, Scientology, Hare Krishna, Zen, Edgar Cayce, Witchcraft, Black Islam, Transcendental Meditation and The Children of God.

Wallace, T. K. "What's Behind the Occultism Craze?" *Family Weekly,* Feb. 28, 1971, p. 4.

Weldon, John. "A Sampling of the New Religions," *International Review of Mission,* Oct., 1978, pp. 407-426.

Tapes

A number of cassette tapes on the new cults, Eastern .

religion, astrology and the occult, etc. are available from Christian Research Institute (Box 500, San Juan Capistrano, Calif. 92693) and the Institute of Contemporary Christianity (Box A, Oakland, New Jersey 07436).

Research and Information

Spiritual Counterfeits Project (P. O. Box 4308, Berkeley, Calif. 94704) has researched and published a number of articles and other materials on many of the new religious movements.

10

Astrology

Advertisements for membership in the Universe Book Club which have appeared recently in various publications, ask concerning astrology: "Why is it firmly believed by 30 million Americans?"; "How does it control the lives of 30 million Americans?" Other estimates indicate that between 40-50 million people in the United States may dabble in astrology. One cannot escape the fact that its popularity has never been greater. Astrology is related to such diverse subjects as: health, diet, sex, marriage, dating, religion, music, business, occupation, menu—and the list goes on. Recent books on astrology have featured such topics as: *Astrological Birth Control, Astrology and Horse Racing, Your Baby's First Horoscope, Your Dog's Astrological Horoscope, Cat Horoscope Book, Astrology for Teens* and *How to Find Your Mate Through Astrology.* Computers have been programmed to give personalized horoscopes of up to 50 pages and 15,000 words. And on many "college campuses there are 24-hour-a-day computers that turn out horoscopes for the younger generation" (William J. Petersen, *Those Curious New Cults,* p. 13).

Dr. Kurt Koch refers to astrology as "the most widely

spread superstition of our time'' (*Between Christ and Satan*, p. 12). John Godwin furnishes the following information:

> Currently the United States boasts some 10,000 professional and 175,000 part-time astrologers. Their incomes range from an occasional $5.00 to an annual six-figure bracket.

> Their clientele consists of an estimated 20 million people [this estimate is very low], who—during 1969—spent more than $150,000,000 on personal horoscope material. Astrology columns now run in 1,200 of America's 1,750 daily newspapers. Twenty years ago—with twice as many papers on the stands—barely one hundred featured them [*Occult America*, p. 3].

Statistics from other countries reveal Koch's contention to be true. Astrology's influence is certainly not unique to America.

> In Great Britain, more than two-thirds of the adult population read their horoscopes. In France 53 percent read their horoscopes daily; and in Germany the percentage who take astrology somewhat seriously is 63 percent [*Those Curious New Cults*, p. 14].

What is astrology? It might be defined as the art or science which has as its basic belief that the fixed stars, sun, moon and planets have a decisive influence on people and things. John W. Montgomery defines it as "the art of divining fate or the future from the juxtaposition of the sun, moon, and planets" (*Principalities and Powers*, p. 108). Astrology and Spiritualism vie for the claim to being the most ancient. (See *Stars, Signs, and Salvation in the Age of Aquarius*, pp. 11-35 for "The Nature and History of Astrology.")

In the treatment of astrology which follows several important questions are investigated. What has caused its resurgence and popularity? Does astrology really work? What are its problems? What is the biblical perspective on astrology? A bibliography of materials cited and for further study concludes the survey.

Astrology's Resurgence and Popularity

An article in the *Los Angeles Times* was captioned: "Astrology Gaining New Acceptance in Europe—Pastime Once Left for Little Old Ladies Gets Most Serious Look in 300 Years." It went on to report that

> a Paris university professor, Michel Garquelin, traces the astrological revival to three major developments: the collapse of religious faith, a concurrent loss of confidence in pure reason as a guide to action and the spreading interest, particularly among the young, in Oriental mystic cults [November 18, 1971].

Mark Graubard, writing in *Natural History,* also speculated on why astrology was experiencing a resurgence.

> Ours is an age in which romance, sentiment, patriotism, religion, and moral values have either been banished or are derided. To some, life seems to be an oppressive vacuum, frustrating and tormenting man's spiritual needs. This has apparently resulted in a need for faith and a desire to speculate about life's purpose and man's fate, as in affluent, decaying Rome. . . . Astrology, then, seems to satisfy the desire for science as well as the need for faith, for belief in powers that rule and manipulate. Moreover, the triumphs in the exploration of space and the new discoveries of astronomy increase man's appetite for renewed worship of unknown powers [May, 1969, p. 18].

Is there a relationship between astrology and loss of religious faith? Constella (Shirley Spencer), a well-known astrologer, felt "that many of astrology's new converts are refugees from religion: 'We're afraid to say no, no, no, to the bearded man upstairs before we have a substitute' " (*Time,* March 21, 1969, p. 56). Howard Sheldon, astrological consultant, believes that young people relate to astrology because

> unlike religion, it gives concrete answers. They simply don't dig the stand-up, Sunday morning sermons. . . .

It offers kids more security than they can find any place else. I have many young clients who've been through that guru thing, the Jesus movement and drugs before finally finding the Big answers in astrology [*L.A. Times*, March 12, 1972, p. E2].

The most remarkable characteristic of astrology's current popularity is its appeal to the youth of America. Only a decade ago, most devotees were over 40—now the average age is 25 or under. About the only thing that has remained constant is that three out of every four persons who follow astrology are female. Although astrology has appealed to the young people, they have shunned the more scholarly books on the subject for more popular works. This has distressed many astrologers (ibid.).

Does Astrology Really Work?

It is obvious that if astrology did not work at all it would not have any followers. Many writers conclude that astrology works in the same way as good psychological advice.

The good astrologer senses the mood of his client, perceives his problems and finds the most positive way of fitting them into the context of the horoscope. . . . The client might have been better advised to consult a psychiatrist, marriage counselor, physician, lawyer or employment agency [*Time*, March 21, 1969, p. 56].

The greatest problem faced in evaluating astrology is that it is so difficult to prove that it does not work.

There are so many variables and options to play with that the astrologer is always right. Break a leg when your astrologer told you the signs were good, and he can congratulate you on escaping what might have happened had the signs been bad. Conversely, if you go against the signs and nothing happens, the astrologer can insist that you were subconsciously careful because you were forewarned [ibid.].

Dr. John W. Montgomery saw the same problem and made an incisive observation:

> No matter how apparently "off" the portrait, this can be explained away as natal potential which has since been modified by environment or experience. Analytical philosophers rightly emphasize . . . that assertions compatible with any state of affairs whatever say nothing. To say something meaningful, one must at least indicate what could count against it; if no contradiction at all makes a difference to one's claims, then the claims really do not impart any information at all. This seems to be the exact situation with most astrological judgments [*Principalities and Powers*, p. 116].

What about the times when astrologers are right? Does this not prove it a science? No. Two astrologers working with the *same* information have often produced conflicting horoscopes. Why? Because as many astrologers admit, astrology "depends upon an almost mediumistic faculty" (Colin Wilson, *The Occult—A History*, p. 251).

Kurt Koch tells the story of how astrology "worked" for a French psychology student who was writing his thesis at the Sorbonne. He placed a classified ad in the newspaper which advertised that he was an astrologer and would produce a personal horoscope for twenty francs. He received 400 responses. "He gave the same horoscope to all 400 customers, paying no heed to the signs of the Zodiac. His only consideration was the psychological aspect. . . . He received many letters of appreciation . . ." (*Between Christ and Satan*, pp. 16, 17).

Astrology's success may be explained in some cases by demonic influence. This is illustrated in the case of a minister who had his horoscope cast in an effort to debunk astrology. He was amazed to find that its predictions were being fulfilled. This went on for eight years.

> The thought came to him that he had sinned through the experiment, and he had placed himself under the influ-

ence of the powers of darkness. After his repentance he discovered to his surprise that his horoscope was now no longer correct. Through this experiment the minister clearly understood that demonic powers can be active in astrology [ibid., p. 18].

It should also be mentioned that there is some evidence that the heavenly bodies (at least the sun and the moon) do influence man. A team of psychiatric researchers from the medical school of the University of Miami concluded that "outbreaks of murder may be triggered by the moon tugging on 'biological tides' inside the human body. . . ." (*L.A. Times*, May 5, 1972, Part 1, p. 12). But this and similar finds do not prove astrology's contentions.

Astrology's Problems

There are a number of problems presented by the critics of astrology which seriously question its claims. A few of these are presented here.

● A comparison of astrological columns and articles written by different astrologers for a given day or other time period are often in hopeless contradiction (*Those Curious New Cults*, p. 19; *Principalities and Powers*, pp. 114, 115).

● Astrology has not kept up with astronomy with the discovery of additional planets and the precession of the equinoxes.

● Many scientists and scientific associations have denounced astrology as worthless from a scientific standpoint. Some very sharp criticisms have been made. Sarton's statement is one example:

> Astrology was perhaps excusable in the social and spiritual disarray of Hellenistic and Roman days; it is unforgivable today. The professional astrologers of our times are fools or crooks or both, and they ought to be restrained, but who will do it? . . .
>
> Superstitions are like diseases, highly contagious diseases. We should be indulgent to Ptolemy, who had innocently accepted the prejudices endemic in his age

89

and could not foresee their evil consequences, but the modern diffusion of astrological superstitions deserves no mercy, and the newspaper owners who do not hesitate to spread lies for the sake of money should be punished just as one punishes the purveyors of adulterated food [*Ancient Science and Modern Civilization*, pp. 61, 62].

Dr. Montgomery quotes Paul Couderc of the Paris Observatory in his study to determine whether the Sun's position in the Zodiac bears any relationship to musical ability as astrologers claim.

The position of the Sun has absolutely no musical significance. . . . We conclude: the assets of scientific astrology are equal to zero, as is the case with commercialized astrology. This is perhaps unfortunate, but it is a fact [*Principalities and Powers*, p. 114].

Petersen presents a number of other problems.

- Why do only the constellations of the Zodiac have any effect on man? . . .
- What about Eskimos and Laplanders? . . . If they are born north of the Arctic Circle, where no planet or sign of the zodiac can be seen for weeks or even months, they are apparently deprived of a destiny.
- Why are there so many astrologies? . . .
- What about twins? . . . Two babies born at the same time in the same place should have the same destiny. Yet one may die [immediately] in the hospital and the other live to be ninety.
- And why does astrology refer to birth rather than conception? [*Those Curious New Cults*, p. 22].

While astrologers have stock answers for many of these problems, their answers are not satisfying.

Astrology and the Biblical Perspective

Since astrology is treated under the general category of *divination* in the Bible, there are comparatively few references to it. Biblically, astrology involved a twofold repudiation of God. In the first place, it violated God's express command (Deut. 18:9-22), and in the second place, it was inevitably associated with idolatry. Although astrology does not appear to be mentioned explicitly in the list of forbidden divination practices of Deut. 18, the Moloch worship at the head of the list was intimately connected with astrology [F. Kinsley Elder, *The Encyclopedia of Christianity*, I, p. 451].

In his brief article, "Astrology and Your Future," Dr. John Davis made five observations on the Christian and modern astrology.

- Astrology leads to a false concept of the universe and its functions. . . .
- Astrology ultimately leads to idolatry and God's judgment. . . . (cf. II Kings 17:16, 17; 23:5).
- Astrology ultimately leads to psychological imbalance and frustration. It is a wretched form of fatalism. . . .
- Worship of the stars is strictly forbidden in Scripture (Deut. 4:15-19; 17:2-5).
- Astrology and all of its attendant theories ignore the basic Biblical teaching about man's future. . . . Not all of the future is to be known by man. . . . God has already given us all we need to know about the future in the Holy Scriptures [*Brethren Missionary Herald*, July 22, 1972, p. 15].

Do the Scriptures offer any support to astrology or astrologers? The answer is a firm "No!" (see chapter 2 of *Stars, Signs and Salvation in the Age of Aquarius* for an expanded discussion).

Conclusion

A choice must be made. Man may follow astrology or the God who created the sun, moon and stars. The Bible is clear that the Creator is to be consulted and worshiped rather than His creation. The Christian does not need astrology to guide him, his future is in the hands of God!

BIBLIOGRAPHY

"Astrology: Fad and Phenomenon," *Time*, March 21, 1969, pp. 47, 48, 53-56.

Bayly, Joseph. *What About Horoscopes?* Elgin, Ill.: David C. Cook Publishing Co., 1970.

Bjornstad, James and Johnson, Shildes. *Stars, Signs, and Salvation in the Age of Aquarius*. Minneapolis: Bethany Fellowship, Inc., 1971.

Davis, John J. "Astrology and Your Future," *Brethren Missionary Herald*, July 22, 1972, pp. 14, 15.

Elder, F. Kingsley. "Astrology," *The Encyclopedia of Christianity*, I, pp. 451, 452.

Godwin, John. *Occult America*. Garden City, New York: Doubleday and Co., 1972. Astrology treated, pp. 1-24.

Graubard, Mark. "Under the Spell of the Zodiac," *Natural History*, May, 1969, pp. 10-18.

Koch, Kurt. *Between Christ and Satan*. Grand Rapids: Kregel Publications, 1962.

Montgomery, John Warwick. *Principalities and Powers*. Minneapolis: Bethany Fellowship, Inc., 1973.

Petersen, William J. *Those Curious New Cults*. New Canaan, Connecticut: Keats Publishing, Inc., 1973. Astrology treated, pp. 13-25.

Sarton, George. *Ancient Science and Modern Civilization*. New York: Harper and Row, 1959.

Wilson, Colin. *The Occult—A History*. New York: Random House, 1971.

11
Baha'i

"No cult bears a gospel better suited to the temper of our times than Baha'i," wrote Charles W. Ferguson (*The Confusion of Tongues*, p. 231). What was true during the 1920's is even more evident today. The ecumenical message of Baha'i has received a significant response in recent years, with membership in the United States tripling during the last decade (*The American Baha'i*, April 1973, p. 1), and currently estimated to be over 100,000. The worldwide outreach of the movement is also impressive; it is reported that

> the Baha'i Faith is now firmly established in more than 60,000 localities. More than 14,100 local Spiritual Assemblies have been elected, 870 of them in the United States alone; and Baha'i literature has been translated into more than 501 languages [ibid., p. 2].

A high percentage of recent converts to Baha'i in America is in the fifteen to thirty age bracket, and from minority groups. Worldwide membership of the cult is estimated at over two million, and Baha'i literature states that some authorities have said "that it is the fastest growing world religion." Historian Arnold Toynbee has written that Baha'i might be the religion of the future.

The following survey gives attention to Baha'i history,

teachings, appeal and outreach. Then the Baha'i Faith is reviewed in its attitude toward Christianity and evaluated by the Bible. A brief bibliography concludes the study.

History

The Baha'i Faith is not native to America, but it came on the American scene from Persia (Iran) in force about sixty years ago. The movement originated in 1844 when Mirza 'Ali Muhammad assumed the title of Bab (Persian for "Gate") and announced that he was the forerunner of the World Teacher who would appear to unite mankind and bring a new era of peace. Many were attracted to the Bab and his message. Being alarmed by his popularity and the growth of his following, orthodox Muslims and the government conspired to suppress the new movement. The Bab was arrested and later executed by a firing squad in 1850. The persecution of the movement continued and more than twenty thousand of his followers were killed, and many were imprisoned.

In 1863, one of the Bab's disciples, Mirza Husayn 'Ali, while an exile in Baghdad, proclaimed himself to be the promised World Teacher and he took the name Baha'u'llah ("The Glory of God"), from which Baha'i is derived (see the historical note at the end of the chapter). Baha'u'llah remained an exile and prisoner until the time of his death in 1892. He designated as his successor his eldest son, 'Abbas Effendi, who assumed the name 'Abdul'l-Baha ("Servant of Baha"). After release from prison in 1908, 'Abdul'l-Baha made several missionary journeys and searched for a suitable location for the first Baha'i Temple. In 1912 he spent eight months in America at which time the cornerstone of the Temple at Wilmette, Illinois was laid.

When 'Abdul'l-Baha died in 1921 he left a will designating his eldest grandson, Shogi Effendi, as his successor. "Under thirty-six years of Shogi Effendi's direction the Baha'is throughout the world have adopted an administrative order that is an application of Baha'u'llah's teachings for a world order'' (*The American Baha'i*, April 1973, p. 3). Since Shogi Effendi's death in 1957 the Baha'is have been governed by a group called "Hands of the Cause." The world headquarters of the movement is in Haifa, Israel. (Further details of the history of the movement may be found in the books by Ferguson, Bach, Esselmont and Miller which are listed in the bibliography.)

Teachings

The Baha'i booklet, *One God, One Religion, One Mankind,* includes an answer to the question, "What are the Main Teachings of the Baha'i Faith?"

The Baha'i Faith revolves around three basic principles: the oneness of God, the oneness of religion, and the oneness of mankind. God, in His Essence, is unknowable; His Word is made known through His Chosen Messengers. Baha'u'llah's Teachings can be summarized in the following principles:

- The independent search after truth, unfettered by superstition or tradition
- The oneness of the entire human race, the pivotal principle and fundamental doctrine of the Faith
- The basic unity of all religions
- The condemnation of all forms of prejudice, whether religious, racial, class or national
- The harmony which must exist between religion and science
- The equality of men and women, the two wings on which the bird of human kind is able to soar
- The introduction of compulsory education
- The adoption of a universal auxiliary language
- The abolition of the extremes of wealth and poverty
- The institution of a world tribunal for the adjudication of disputes between nations
- The exaltation of work, performed in the spirit of service, to the rank of worship
- The glorification of justice as the ruling principle in human society, and of religion as a bulwark for the

protection of all peoples and nations.
- The establishment of a permanent and universal peace as the supreme goal of all mankind

This Baha'i statement emphasizes "oneness" and "unity" in the religious, social and political realms. The practical aspects of Baha'i are much like the aims of many modern clergymen, sociologists, politicians and other leaders.

In dealing with the subject, "What is a Baha'i?" Esslemont explains:

> In order to attain the Baha'i life *in all its fullness,* conscious and direct relations with Baha'u'llah are as necessary as is sunshine for the unfolding of the lily or rose. The Baha'i worships not the human personality of Baha'u'llah, but the Glory of God manifest through that personality. He reverences Christ and Muhammad and all God's former Messengers to mankind, but he recognizes Baha'u'llah as the Bearer of God's Message for the new age in which we live, as the Great World-teacher who has come to carry on and consummate the work of his predecessors [*Baha'u'llah and the New Era,* pp. 91, 92].

This is the crux: While speaking of unifying all religions, the Baha'is ask persons to accept another prophet, Baha'u'llah, as the one who supersedes all the others. A study of Baha'i teachings reveals that most are antithetical to biblical Christianity.

Appeal

In his article, "A New Look at Baha'i," James Moore summarized Baha'i appeal to converts as viewed by Salvatore A. Pelle, Director of Public Information at Baha'i National Headquarters:

> . . . "The inhumanity perpetrated in the name of Christianity, an outdated Biblical revelation and a scientifically untenable doctrine of the incarnation cause

today's youth to reject Christianity automatically." His "barrier breaking" religion, claims Pelle, will appeal to these spiritual rebels because the faith: 1) "fits the twentieth century" with a new revelation through Baha'u'llah which updates the Bible; 2) makes sense of the common element in the teachings of all religions by declaring that "all true religions come from the same Divine Source," and that "truth is continuous and relative, not final and absolute"; 3) refuses to define God, referring to Him as "Unknowable Essence"; 4) teaches as its fundamental doctrine the oneness of the entire race [*His,* February 1971, p. 17].

Other features of the Baha'i Faith which are attractive to converts include:

- its concern for the social and political problems of mankind
- its high standard of moral conduct
- its absence of a professional clergy
- its emphasis on the active involvement of every member
- its aggressive missionary program

Outreach

Baha'i is a missionary religion. Individual Baha'is accept the responsibility for promoting their faith by holding meetings ("Firesides") in their homes. Public gatherings are also sponsored. Hundreds of volunteer teachers, called "pioneers," leave their communities and set up new residences at home or abroad for the purpose of propagating Baha'i where it is not well known. Missionary work during the past fifty years has opened hundreds of countries and smaller political and geographical units to Baha'i.

In some areas Baha'i has experienced remarkable growth. For example, in South Vietnam, the Baha'i community grew from 40,000 in 1968 to 121,000 at the present time. In the deep south, during several weeks in 1970, almost 8,000 rural blacks became Baha'is (*The American Baha'i,* April 1973, pp. 1, 10). Thousands of new converts have also been made in California, Illinois and New York.

J. K. Van Baalen viewed the beautiful Wilmette Temple as Baha'i's chief means of propaganda outreach in the United States (*The Chaos of Cults*, 4th rev. ed., p. 152). Built at a cost of three million dollars, it was formally dedicated in 1953. Other Baha'i temples have been built in Sydney, Australia; Kampala, Uganda; Frankfurt, Germany; and Panama City, Panama. The only architectural requirement for each of the temples is that it have nine sides, surmounted by a dome. "Its nine entrances symbolize the unity of religion and the oneness of mankind" (*One God, One Religion, One Mankind*).

Extensive use has been made of the printed page, and Baha'i materials have been translated into hundreds of languages. All the evidence points toward an increasing encounter between Christianity and the Baha'i Faith.

Baha'i, Christianity and the Bible

Can a Christian be a Baha'i? William M. Miller gives the answer.

> It has been supposed by some that a Christian is able to retain his faith and his membership in his church while he joins the Baha'i movement and works for peace and brotherhood and justice for all. Some Christians have attempted to do this. However, Shoghi Effendi and other Baha'i leaders have made it clear that this is not possible. It should be clearly understood that when a Christian becomes a Baha'i he by so doing rejects the basic doctrines of the Bible, denies his Christian faith, and starts off in a different direction . . . [*Incite*, Dec., 1975, p. 28].

As William J. Petersen so aptly put it, "Baha'i collides head-on with Christianity; it isn't a pleasant merger" (*Those Curious New Cults*, p. 189). Baha'i teachers do not seek to emphasize the clash between Christianity and Baha'i; they would rather avoid the conflict. But interviews with them leave no doubt that Baha'i rejects all the cardinal doctrines of historic biblical Christianity: the Trinity, Deity of Christ, Virgin Birth, Bodily Resurrection of Christ, Substitutionary Atonement, salvation by faith, final authority of the Bible and the Second Advent of Christ. (See Martin's interview with a Baha'i teacher, *The Kingdom of the Cults,* pp. 254-257.)

A Bible-believing Christian cannot accept the view that Jesus Christ is adequately represented in Baha'i because He is given *a* place. Scripturally, He must be given *first place*, to the *exclusion of all others*. The acceptance of the claims of Baha'u'llah forces a rejection of many passages of the Bible having any current application to Jesus Christ. For example:

> John 14:6: "Jesus saith unto him, I am the way, the truth, and the life: no man cometh unto the Father, but by me."
>
> Acts 4:12: "Neither is there salvation in any other: for there is none other name under heaven given among men, whereby we must be saved."
>
> I Corinthians 3:11: "For other foundation can no man lay than that is laid, which is Jesus Christ."
>
> I Timothy 2:5: "For *there is* one God, and one mediator between God and men, the man Christ Jesus."
>
> Hebrews 13:8: "Jesus Christ the same yesterday, and to-day, and for ever."

Baha'i robs the Christian of the "blessed hope" of the Second Coming of Jesus Christ:

> If you are of the Christian Faith which had its origin approximately the year 1, your prophecy concerning the return of Christ in the glory of the Father has been fulfilled. His new name in this day is Baha'u'llah which means the Glory of God" [*L.A. Times,* October 22, 1971].

This "fulfillment" does not agree with what Scripture demands: "Looking for that blessed hope, and the glorious appearing of the great God and our Saviour Jesus Christ" (Titus 2:13). At the Ascension the apostles were told by the angels that "this same Jesus, which is taken up from you into heaven, shall so come in like manner as ye have seen him go into heaven" (Acts 1:11).

Baha'i's teachings of "the oneness of religion" is not a biblical concept. While all religions have certain basic elements in common, Christianity cannot compromise its teachings to accommodate the doctrines set forth by Hinduism, Buddhism, Muhammadanism, or any other religion. None of them, including Baha'i, accept the Bible's teaching concerning man's sin and the relationship of the work of Christ to man's redemption (Rom. 3:23; Isa. 64:6; John 1:29; 3:14-17).

Conclusion

Baha'i does not, nor can it, offer any present hope of sins forgiven and a sure standing before God. In fact Baha'i views such a claim as presumptuous (*The Kingdom of the Cults*, p. 256). John presents a different picture:

> And this is the record, that God hath given to us eternal life, and this life is in his Son. He that hath the Son hath life; and he that hath not the Son of God hath not life. These things have I written unto you that believe on the name of the Son of God; that ye may know that ye have eternal life, and that ye may believe on the name of the Son of God [I John 5:11-13].

BIBLIOGRAPHY

Bach, Marcus. *They Have Found a Faith*. New York: The Bobbs-Merrill Co., 1946. Baha'i treated, pp. 189-221.

Ferguson, Charles W. *The Confusion of Tongues*. Garden City, New York: Doubleday, Doran and Co., 1928. Baha'i treated, pp. 231-250.

Martin, Walter R. *The Kingdom of the Cults*, Rev. ed.;

Minneapolis: Bethany Fellowship, Inc., 1965. Baha'i treated, pp. 252-258.

Miller, William M. *The Baha'i Faith: Its History and Teachings*. S. Pasadena, Calif.: William Carey Library, 1974. This book is also available in an abridgment by William N. Wysham, *What is the Baha'i Faith?* Wm. B. Eerdmans Publishing Co., 1977.

————. "What is the Baha'i World Faith?" *Incite,* Dec., 1975, pp. 22-28. (Available in booklet form from CARIS, P. O. Box 1783, Santa Ana, Calif. 92702.)

Moore, James. "A New Look at Baha'i," *His,* Feb., 1971, pp. 16-18.

Petersen, William J. *Those Curious New Cults*. New Canaan, Connecticut: Keats Publishing, Inc., 1973. Baha'i treated, pp. 181-191.

Van Baalen, J. K. *The Chaos of Cults*. 4th rev. ed.; Wm. B. Eerdmans Publishing Co., 1962. Baha'i treated, pp. 146-161.

Baha'i Materials

Materials may be obtained through local Baha'i centers or by writing to the National Baha'i Administrative Headquarters, 536 Sheridan Road, Wilmette, Illinois 60091.

The American Baha'i is published monthly by the National Spiritual Assembly of the Baha'is of the United States.

Esslemont, J. E. *Baha'u'llah and the New Era*. Rev. ed.; Wilmette, Illinois: The Baha'i Publishing Committee, 1950. The Preface states that it is "a trustworthy introduction to the history and teachings of the Baha'i Faith."

Historical Note

William M. Miller, who served as a missionary in Iran for 43 years, did some extensive research on the Babi-Baha'i movement and its literature. It is his conclusion that much of the current Baha'i literature does not give an accurate account of the history and teachings of the movement according to the best available material (*Incite,* Dec., 1975, p. 23).

For example, the claim that Baha'u'llah is the latest "Manifestation," or prophet of God, and that the Bab was his forerunner is historically suspect, for as Miller points out, "The Bab claimed to be the greatest Manifestation who had come, but he would not be the last. After him yet another would come much greater than he. . . . Though he did not predict the exact time of the appearing of the next Manifestation, he assumed that it would not occur for many centuries. He specifically mentioned 1,511 and 2,001 years in the future as dates within which the Manifestations would appear (Bayan II, 17). And after that still other Manifestations would appear in the millenniums yet to come!" (ibid., p. 23).

With this background, it is easy to understand why the public announcement of Mirza Husayn'Ali (about 1866) that *he* was the new Manifestation predicted by the Bab surprized the Babi community and why some rejected his claim (ibid., p. 24). Baha'u'llah "adopted the Bab's doctrine of Manifestations, but he referred to the Bab not so much as a major manifestation but as a 'forerunner' of his. He indicated that the Bab had the same relation to him that John the Baptist had to Christ" (ibid., p. 24). The book by Miller listed in the bibliography is an in depth study of the history and theology of the Baha'i faith.

12
Rosicrucianism

"WHAT SECRET POWER DID THIS MAN POS-
SESS?" reads the caption. The advertisement continues:

> WHY was this man great? How does anyone—man or
> woman—achieve greatness? Is it not by mastery of the
> powers within ourselves?

> Know the mysterious world within you! Attune yourself
> to the wisdom of the ages! Grasp the inner power of your
> mind! Learn the secrets of a full and peaceful life!
> Benjamin Franklin—like many other learned and great
> men and women—was a Rosicrucian. . . .

This statement epitomizes the appeal and goal of Rosicrucianism. The reader of the ad is invited to write for a free
copy of *The Mastery of Life*. The book presents the Rosicrucian philosophy, a brief treatment on the history of the Order,
the benefits of membership, and an invitation to unite with
the Ancient Mystical Order Rosae Crucis, usually abbre-
viated to AMORC. Located in San Jose, California, this is
the most widely known of the Rosicrucian societies.

A rival California body, The Rosicrucian Fellowship,
founded by Max Heindel (1865-1919), has its center in
Oceanside. Another Rosicrucian group, The Church of the
Illumination, was organized in 1908, and has its center of

operation in Quakertown, Pennsylvania. Recently this writer became aware of another group which operated in California, Lectorium Rosicrucianum, with headquarters in Haarlem, The Netherlands. The Rosicrucian movement, like many other occult-oriented groups, has experienced rapid growth in recent years, and it is estimated that there are currently over 250,000 Rosicrucians in America.

Charles Braden characterized Rosicrucianism as it is found in the world today:

> There are Rosicrucian societies, fraternities, orders, fellowships or lodges in most countries of the modern world. Some of them are very active; others are obscure and highly secret; some seem primarily religious in their emphasis, and some categorically deny that Rosicrucianism is a religion, holding rather that it is a philosophy, making use of the most modern scientific methods and techniques, as well as the methods of the occultist, the mystic and the seer, in the quest for truth.

> But, while Rosicrucianism is sectarian in character and the various branches are sometimes bitterly critical of each other, they do have common features, the central one being the purported possession of certain secret wisdom handed down from ancient times, through a secret brotherhood, an esoteric wisdom that can only be imparted to the initiated [''Rosicrucianism,'' *Encyclopaedia Britannica,* 1964 ed., XIX, p. 558].

What is the historical origin of Rosicrucianism? What are some of the basic Rosicrucian teachings? Why are people drawn to the movement? How is the Order to be evaluated? The Rosicrucian Order primarily in view in this survey is AMORC, San Jose.

History

H. Spencer Lewis, AMORC's First Imperator for North and South America, between 1915 and 1939, claimed that Rosicrucianism began in ancient Egypt, a view that is also propagated in *Mastery of Life:* ''. . . The Order had its birth as one of the mystery schools of secret wisdom in ancient Egypt during the 18th Dynasty, or the reign of Pharaoh Amenhotep IV, about 1350 B.C.'' (12th ed., p. 16). It is also claimed that such movements as the Essenes and the early Christian church itself—and such individuals as Jesus, Plato and Philo—were related to the Rosicrucian Order. But non-Rosicrucian scholars are not so convinced.

There is much controversy and obscurity surrounding the early history of the Rosicrucians. It is taught that Christian Rosenkreuz (''Rosy Cross''—1378-1484) was the founder. The story of his search for knowledge and true wisdom, and the founding of the Order was published in 1614, in the famous *Fama Fraternitatis*. This document tells how Rosenkreuz traveled in Damascus, Damcar (Arabia?), Egypt and Fez, where he came into the possession of much secret wisdom. Then he journeyed to Spain, but being disappointed with his reception there, he returned to Germany where he imparted his knowledge first to three disciples and then to four others, and the Order was established. While many hold to the historicity of Christian Rosenkreuz, it is generally held that he was not a real person at all, but rather a legendary or symbolic character used for the mythical explanation of the Order. Two other works appeared after the *Fama* which gave it further publicity: *Confessio Fraternitatis Rosae Crucis* (1615) and the *Chemical Wedding of Christian Rosenkreuz* (1616). (For further details on Rosicrucian history see *Secret Societies,* pp. 109-127.)

Many authors have suggested various meanings which might be associated with the rose and the cross which are used as an emblem by the Rosicrucians. H. Spencer Lewis (AMORC) wrote that ''a book might be written upon the Symbology or Mystical meaning of the Rose and the Cross'' (*Rosicrucian Manual,* 10th ed., 1947, p. 42). Then he explained:

In our Work, the Cross represents many things esoterically; likewise the Rose. But exoterically, the Rose represents *Secrecy* and Evolution, while the Cross represents the Labors and Burdens of Life and the karma which we must endure in our earthly existence [ibid.].

Rosicrucian writers do not comprehend the true meaning of the Cross which finds its significance, not in man's evolutionary development, but in *God's* provision of salvation through the death of Christ, "Who his own self bare our sins in his own body on the tree, that we, being dead to sins, should live unto righteousness: by whose stripes ye were healed" (I Pet. 2:24).

Teachings

Rosicrucianism is a complicated system of thought and it is difficult to extract a complete statement of beliefs. Walter R. Martin says that it

is not only an eclectic theological system which mixes pagan mythology with Judaism and Christianity with traces of Hinduism and Buddhism throughout, but it is a system of thinking which seeks to synthesize the basic truths of all religions and absorb them into a master system.

In the literature of Rosicrucianism one will find enormous deposits of symbolism, anthropology, transmigration and even some spiritism.

There is great similarity in some areas for the vocabulary of theosophy and to the concept that man progresses through many reincarnations, each of which purges him of his preceding sins [*The Kingdom of the Cults,* rev. ed., p. 428].

While they take the position that they are not a religious organization, the Rosicrucians do a thorough job of contradicting every major teaching of orthodox Christianity. For example:
- God is considered as an impersonal being;
- The Trinity "becomes a type of occult pantheism";

- the unique deity of Christ is rejected along with the vicarious atonement;
- reincarnation is substituted for resurrection; and
- man is viewed as evolving into a divine being (ibid., 430-432).

As a sample of the perversion of biblical Christianity set forth in Rosicrucian books, a few brief quotations are cited from H. Spencer Lewis' *The Mystical Life of Jesus* (8th ed., 1948). This book is advertised as the "Most Surprising Book Ever Printed."

- Lewis writes that "Jesus was born of *Gentile* parents through whose veins flowed Aryan blood" (p. 53).
- He claims that Jesus' words from the Cross "could not mean, 'My God, My God, why hast thou forsaken me?' but rather 'My Temple of Helois, My Brethren of Helois, why has thou forsaken me?' " (p. 263).
- Jesus did not die on the Cross, for "an examination of the body revealed that Jesus was *not dead*. The blood *flowing from the wounds* proved that his body was not lifeless. . . " (p. 265).
- The Ascension is rejected because "there is nothing in the original accounts of it to warrant the belief that Jesus arose physically or in His physical body in a cloud into the Heavens" (p. 283).
- And finally, it is claimed that Rosicrucian archival records "clearly show that after Jesus retired to the monastery at Carmel He lived for many years, and carried on secret missions with His Apostles . . ." (p. 289).

This book is filled with similar extra-biblical "revelations," all in violent disagreement with what the Bible says. The book might more accurately be titled: *The Mythical Life of Jesus!*

In this same volume a number of other books in the Rosicrucian Library are advertised. Among these, listed as Volume XV, is *The Book of Jasher* (p. 328), which is supposed to be the lost book mentioned in the Bible (Josh.

10:13; II Sam. 1:18). The advertisement carries the indignant questions:

> BY WHAT right has man been denied the words of the prophets? Who dared expunge from the Holy Bible one of its inspired messages? For centuries man has labored under the illusion that there have been preserved for him the collected books of the great teachers and disciples— yet one has been withheld—''The Book of Jasher.''

Dr. Edgar J. Goodspeed included the *Book of Jasher* in his work, *Modern Apocrypha* (retitled *Famous "Biblical" Hoaxes*), and exposed the very rendition republished by the Rosicrucians, as a literary fraud. It had already been so exposed in the eighteenth and nineteenth centuries. Goodspeed concluded: ''The Book of Jasher, as they have published it, is no older than 1750'' (p. 87). How many other ''authoritative'' records in the Rosicrucian archives suffer from this or like defects?

Appeal

Much of Rosicrucianism's appeal is to be found in its accent on the occult and the mysterious. Rosicrucian literature also promises the person answers to all his problems and the realization of his full potential. The one interested in uniting with the Rosicrucian Order (AMORC) is advised of the many benefits such membership can afford him in *Mastery of Life* (12th ed., pp. 21-28):

- A system of guidance (lessons and home study);
- A lodge at home (''Your Home is Your Temple'');
- Demonstrations—simple experiments (''Many are not of a physical nature but rather are *mental* experiments'');
- Signs of recognition (membership card, passwords, grips, symbolic initiations);
- A fascinating monthly magazine, *The Rosicrucian Digest*;
- Personal attention;
- Various departmental facilities (correspondence, research library, etc.);

• Intimate association with other Rosicrucians.

This writer believes that many are attracted to the cult because of the statement, "The Rosicrucians are NOT a religious organization." The emphasis on Rosicrucianism being a philosophy and not a religion permits many church members to join.

Evaluation

Even a cursory investigation of Rosicrucian teachings makes it clear that they are basically anti-Christian, if the Bible is accepted as the standard. J. K. Van Baalen evaluated the Rosicrucian system as one

> that denies and perverts everything taught by Christ and concerning Christ. . . .

> . . . The entire structure is built upon a false foundation, namely, another than the Christ of the Scriptures.

> The crowning test of a religious or philosophical system of thought . . . must always be: How do its statements compare with what has been held to be in harmony with the Scripture by the entire Christian Church? When we do this, we reach the conclusion that the Apostle Paul would say of the followers of the Rose Cross that they are "enemies of the cross of Christ" [*The Chaos of Cults*, 4th rev. ed., pp. 121, 122].

After a study of Rosicrucian teachings one can understand why Walter R. Martin claims that "everything Christian that it touches suffers violence at its hands" (*The Kingdom of the Cults*, rev. ed., p. 429).

Joyce Blackwell, a former Rosicrucian, stated that because Rosicrucians "said their teachings were an extension of the Bible," she didn't realize immediately after becoming a Christian that their doctrines "were actually anti-Christian." This contradiction between Rosicrucianism and the Bible became clear after studying the Scriptures. "After Bible class one night I said, 'There is a terrible discrepancy between the Rosicrucian teaching and what the Bible teaches' '' (James R. Adair and Ted Miller, *We Found Our Way Out,* pp. 31, 32).

Conclusion

This brief survey has made it obvious that historic biblical Christianity and Rosicrucianism are *incompatible*. The Bible expresses the warning God gives to those who follow a system apart from that revealed in Scripture. "There is a way which seemeth right unto a man; but the end thereof *are* the ways of death" (Prov. 14:12).

BIBLIOGRAPHY

Adair, James R. and Miller, Ted. *We Found Our Way Out*. Grand Rapids: Baker Book House, 1964. "I Was a Rosicrucian," by Joyce Blackwell, pp. 27-34.

Braden, Charles S. "Rosicrucianism," *Encyclopaedia Britannica* (1964 ed.), XIX, p. 558.

Daraul, Arkon. *A History of Secret Societies*. New York: Pocket Books, 1961. "The Rosicrucians" treated, pp. 226-239.

Goodspeed, Edgar J. *Famous "Biblical" Hoaxes*. Grand Rapids: Baker Book House, 1956. "The Book of Jasher" is dealt with on pp. 81-87.

Howe, Ellic. "Rosicrucians," *Man, Myth and Magic,* number 87, pp. 2425-2433.

MacKenzie, Norman (ed.). *Secret Societies*. New York: Collier Books, 1971. "The Rosicrucians" treated, pp. 109-127.

Martin, Walter R. *The Kingdom of the Cults*. Rev. ed.; Minneapolis: Bethany Fellowship, Inc., 1965. "The Rosicrucian Fellowship" treated, pp. 428-432.

Mayer, F. E. *The Religious Bodies of America*. 4th rev. ed.; St. Louis, Mo.: Concordia Publishing House, 1961. See pp. 555-560.

Van Baalen, J. K. *The Chaos of Cults*. 4th rev. ed.; Grand

Rapids: Wm. B. Eerdmans Publishing Co., 1962. "Rosicrucianism" treated, pp. 104-127.

Rosicrucian Materials

Rosicrucian materials are readily available from the Rosicrucian Fellowship, Oceanside, California and The Rosicrucians (AMORC), Rosicrucian Park, San Jose, California. Key Rosicrucian writers include R. Swinburne Clymer, Max Heindel and H. Spencer Lewis. Their works are too numerous to list.

13

The Occult and
the Ouija Board

The occult (from the Latin: *that which is hidden, covered, mysterious*) holds a strong fascination for many people in America today. While millions are involved in occult practices, such participation is not supported by the Bible (Lev. 19:31; 20:6; Deut. 18:10, 11; II Chron. 33:6; Isa. 8:19-20; 47:13, 14). At Ephesus, the manifestation of the power of Jesus Christ (Acts 19:11-17) brought a departure from occult involvement:

> And many that believed came, and confessed, and showed their deeds. Many of them also which used curious [magical] arts brought their books together, and burned them before all *men:* and they counted the price of them, and found *it* fifty thousand *pieces* of silver [vs. 18, 19].

Persons attuned to Bible Christianity forsake the occult. At Ephesus a price was paid, the value of the materials destroyed was at least $10,000.

One important aspect of "Occult America" is the use of the Ouija board. I became interested in this device because of its frequent mention by young people and the questions which they asked about it. Periodically, pastors wrote to me asking for information on the *board*. My interest was further stimulated when my son gave a presentation on "The Occult" at school. The teacher of the class thought it unusual that I would not let my son "play" with the *board;* after all, reasoned the teacher, "It was just a game." My study of Ouija board history and the cases of many users who encountered great difficulties through *board* use, proved this common opinion wrong.

Information on the Ouija board is needed in this day when its popularity is so great. What is its history? What makes it work? Are there any dangers in its use? What should the Christian's attitude be toward it?

History of the Board

Writers state that devices similar to the Ouija board were known to the Egyptians and other ancient peoples. Psychical researcher, Nandor Fodor, indicated that an instrument like the Ouija board "was in use in the days of Pythagoras, about 540 B.C." (*Encyclopaedia of Psychic Science,* p. 270). The fourth century Byzantine historian, Ammianus Marcellinus gave a detailed account of divination which employed a pendulum and the letters of the alphabet which were engraved on the rim of a round metal dish. A less sophisticated method of divination used by the Romans made use of a ring which was suspended by a hair or thread, in or within reach of a glass vessel. Answers to questions were obtained when the ring struck the glass in response to a predetermined code, or when the correct letters of the alphabet were recited. Table-tipping (in practice more a table-rapping), while used in ancient times and during the Middle Ages, came into popular use during the nineteenth century. In addition to response through raps for "yes" and "no," the letters of the alphabet were also recited and the table responded at the appropriate letters, and sentences could be spelled out.

In 1853, M. Planchett, a French spiritualist, invented the "planchette," a small heart-shaped table with three legs, one of which was a lead-pencil. The operator's fingers were placed lightly on top of it and when the instrument worked it moved over the top of a piece of paper and wrote out messages. A cognate method of communication is automatic writing, where the subject sits with a pencil in hand and after a time writes "automatically."

The Ouija board was born when the pencil of the planchette was replaced by a third leg and an alphabet board replaced the paper. The invention of the Ouija board in 1889 (patented in 1892) is credited to William Fuld of Baltimore, Maryland. With some minor variations the Ouija board is a rectangular board about eighteen inches long and twelve wide. On it are printed the words "yes" and "no" and "goodbye." The message indicator is a small, plastic, heart-shaped table about six inches long. The three legs of the indicator are felt-tipped so that they slide easily under the light fingertip touch of one or two operators. *Board* sales increased during the First World War and its popularity reached a peak in 1920. It again became popular in 1944 during the Second World War. The most recent interest in the occult also brought a surge in Ouija sales. The patents on the *board* were purchased in 1966 by Parker Brothers of Salem, Massachusetts. Surprisingly, in 1967, the Ouija board became America's favorite board "game," and it was reported that sales were about two million. How long this popularity will be sustained only time will tell.

What Makes it Work?

Parker Brothers, manufacturers of the Ouija Board, offer no solution to what makes the board work, stating that "how or why it works is a mystery . . ." (*The Weird and Wonderful Ouija Talking Board Set*, p. 2). At least three explanations have been given.

• Imperceptible muscular movements cause the indicator to move and the messages originate in the conscious or subconscious mind of the operator.

• Much is interpreted as conscious or subconscious as to source, but a smaller portion derives from contact with the spirits of the disincarnate dead.

• Much comes through the conscious and subconscious mind of the operator, but a smaller portion is contact with evil spirits (demons). This view of Ouija board phenomena held by most Christians, rejects the spiritualist interpretation because the Bible does not allow for the wandering about of disincarnate spirits (II Cor. 5:8; Phil. 1:23; Luke 23:43; John 14:2). Some authors state that any attempt at present to deny the possible intrusion of the supernatural into Ouija board use is premature, for as John Godwin points out, "the entire spectrum of automatism remains largely unexplored" (John Godwin, *Occult America,* p. 273).

The Ouija board should be seen as a device which sometimes actually makes contact with the supernatural for several reasons.

• The content of the messages often goes beyond that which can be reasonably explained as coming from the conscious or subconscious mind of the operator. Examples of such are presented in Sir William F. Barrett's *On the Threshold of the Unseen* (pp. 176-189), and in the experiences of Mrs. John H. Curran, related in the book *Singer in the Shadows*.

• The many cases of "possession" after a period of Ouija board use also support the claim that supernatural contact is made through the *board*. Psychics and parapsychologists have received letters from hundreds of people who have experienced "possession" (an invasion of their personalities). Rev. Donald Page, a well-known clairvoyant and exorcist of the Christian Spiritualist Church is reported as saying that most of his "possession" cases "are people who have used the Ouija board," and that "this is one of the

115

easiest and quickest ways to become possessed" (*Man, Myth and Magic,* number 73, after p. 2060). While Page views these "possessions" as caused by disincarnate entities, the reality of possession is still clear. The Christian sees the invader as an evil spirit (demon).

• The *board* has been subjected to tests which support supernatural intervention. The testing of the *board* was presented in an article by Sir William Barrett, in the September 1914 *Proceedings of the American Society for Psychical Research* (pp. 381-394). The Barrett report indicated that the *board* worked efficiently with the operators blindfolded, the *board's* alphabet rearranged and its surface hidden from the sight of those working it. It worked with such speed and accuracy under these tests that Barrett concluded:

> Reviewing the results as a whole I am convinced of their supernormal character, and that we have here an exhibition of some intelligent, disincarnate agency, mingling with the personality of one or more of the sitters and guiding their muscular movements [p. 394].

In his book, *On the Threshold of the Unseen,* Barrett referred to these same experiences and stated: ". . . Whatever may have been the source of the intelligence displayed, it was absolutely beyond the range of any normal human faculty" (p. 181). Similar statements could be multiplied.

The fact remains that the Ouija board works. Much phenomena is certainly through conscious and subconscious activity, but that some is of supernatural character must be accepted.

Potential Dangers

There are potential dangers in the use of the Ouija board as a game or as an approach to "psychic development." As the operator becomes more involved with the *board* his fascination with it often leads him to dependence and to the surrender of his will. After a time the answers to the questions asked are anticipated in the mind before they are spelled out on the *board*. After this the *board* may be discarded, and in its place the operator may hear a voice. Sometimes the *voice* (often more than one) communicates almost continuously and the messages are often profane and obscene. Beyond this, sensual feelings, sexual stimulation and the use of the person's vocal cords for expression by the "possessing entity" (demon) may also take place.

G. Godfrey Raupert explained from his observations how occult entrapment often came about, and warned of tragic results.

> Suggestions are made in the most subtle manner, in exalted language, appealing to the youthful imagination and to dangerous tendencies latent in all men; and when it is borne in mind that the invisible counsellor who makes these suggestions is believed to be a kindly father or mother who could only desire the well-being of her child, and that the experimenter's power of discrimination is lost, one can imagine how far this kind of mischief can be carried.

> As the "psychic development" advances, the entire mental and moral nature of the experimenter becomes disordered; and he discovers to his cost that, while it was an easy thing for him to *open* the mental door by which the mind could be invaded, it is a difficult, if not an impossible thing, to *shut* that door and to expel the invader. For the impulse to communicate or to write now asserts itself imperatively and incessantly, at all hours of the day and in the midst of every kind of occupation, and, in the end, even at night, either suddenly awakening the victim or preventing him from securing any refreshing sleep. A pitiable condition of mental and moral collapse, often terminating in suicide or insanity, is frequently the ultimate result [*The Ecclesiastical Review,* Nov., 1918, pp. 474, 475].

Statements which warn of the dangers of Ouija board experimentation have been made by psychologists, psychiatrists, medical doctors, theologians and many other informed persons. While they do not always agree on the source of the danger (whether psychological, disincarnate spirit, or demon) they all agree that dangers do exist. If space permitted dozens of statements could be cited.

Dr. Carl Wickland (M.D.) explained how he was drawn into psychical research.

> The serious problem of alienation and mental derangement attending ignorant psychic experiments was first brought to my attention by the cases of several persons whose seemingly harmless experiences with automatic writing and the Ouija board resulted in such wild insanity that commitment to asylums was necessitated. . . .

> Many other disastrous results which followed the use of the supposedly innocent Ouija board came to my notice and my observations led me into research in psychic phenomena for a possible explanation of these strange occurrences [*Thirty Years Among the Dead*, pp. 16, 17].

Unfortunately, he later came to accept the spiritualist explanation of the phenomena.

Pastor H. Richard Neff concluded that for the most part the Ouija board worked because of autosuggestion, but he also warned:

> A sufficient number of people have got into serious psychological difficulty through use of a Ouija board to warn us that these instruments may not be "innocent toys." Most serious students of parapsychology strongly advise people not to use Ouija boards and such instruments [*Psychic Phenomena and Religion*, p. 131].

The Guide Book for the Study of Psychical Research, under "Ouija Board," in the Glossary, says:

> Many researchers have pointed out the inherent dangers of using the Ouija board or of taking its "messages" seriously, because of the possibility of dredging up some very unpleasant and potentially disturbing attitudes and facts from one's subconscious. There have been numerous instances of persons who have become very upset emotionally from the use of the Ouija board [p. 182].

The potential dangers of Ouija board experimentation, here only touched upon, are evident and require no additional comment.

Conclusion

What should the Christian's attitude be toward the Ouija board? Obviously, he should not use it because:

The Bible condemns occult involvement (Lev. 19:31; 20:6);

The tragic experiences of many who have been involved argue against it;

Its messages are often false, obscene and contrary to Bible truth.

Where the Christian is to go for his guidance, understanding and wisdom is clear in the Scripture:

> And when they shall say unto you, Seek unto them that have familiar spirits, and unto wizards that peep and that mutter: should not a people seek unto their God? . . . [Isa. 8:19].

> If any of you lack wisdom, let him ask of God, that giveth to all *men* liberally, and upbraideth not; and it shall be given him [James 1:5].

Writing during a former period of Ouija board popularity, Pastor I. M. Haldeman made the Christian position plain: "No more think of having a Ouija board in your home or fooling with it . . . than you would invite the arch-enemy of God and man to dwell intimately with you" (*Can the Dead Communicate with the Living?*, p. 116).

BIBLIOGRAPHY

Barrett, W. F. "On Some Experiments with the Ouija Board and Blindfolded Sitters," *Proceedings of the American Society for Psychical Research,* Sept., 1914, pp. 381-394.

―――. *On the Threshold of the Unseen.* New York: E. P. Dutton and Co., 1918. Chapter 14 is titled: "Proof of Super-Normal Messages: The Ouija Board."

Fodor, Nandor. "Ouija Board," *Encyclopaedia of Psychic Science*. New Hyde Park, New York: University Books, Inc. 1966.

Godwin, John. *Occult America*. Garden City, New York: Doubleday and Co., Inc., 1972.

Gruss, Edmond C. *The Ouija Board: Doorway to the Occult*. Chicago: Moody Press, 1975. A complete treatment on the subject. Available from the author for $2.00 postpaid.

————. *What About the Ouija Board?* Chicago: Moody Press, 1973. An Acorn booklet.

Litvag, Irving. *Singer in the Shadows,* New York: The Macmillan Co., 1972. One of the most unusual of Ouija Board experiences.

"Ouija, Ouija, Who's Got the Ouija?" *The Literary Digest,* July 3, 1920, pp. 66-68. Contains a brief history of the Ouija board.

Parker Brothers. *The Weird and Wonderful Ouija Talking Board Set*. This brochure is sent by Parker Brothers in response to letters asking questions about the *board*.

Raupert, J. Godfrey. "The Truth About the Ouija Board," *The Ecclesiastical Review,* Nov., 1918, pp. 463-478. A good treatment by a Catholic expert on the subject written during a former period of Ouija popularity.

Strachan, Francoise. "A Company of Devils," *Man, Myth and Magic,* number 73, after p. 2060 (not paginated).

Wright, J. Stafford. *Christianity and the Occult*. Chicago: Moody Press, 1971. Presents a helpful discussion of the occult from a Christian viewpoint.

14

Edgar Cayce
and the A.R.E.

Edgar Cayce (pronounced Casey) has been identified as America's "greatest mystic," "most famous clairvoyant," and "most famous prophet." Jeanne Dixon said that "Cayce was clearly one of the most remarkable psychics who ever lived." He certainly has become one of the most widely publicized psychics of this century. One of the unusual features of Cayce's fame is the fact that it reached its peak *after* his death in 1945.

Numerous questions may be asked concerning Edgar Cayce, his experiences, his psychic readings, the teachings derived from his sleeplike trances, and the work of the Association for Research and Enlightenment, Inc. (A.R.E.). A brief survey of these areas of interest is presented here. A selective bibliography closes the study.

Edgar Cayce

Edgar Cayce was born on a farm near Hopkinsville, Kentucky, in 1877. His grandfather may have had psychic powers for it was reported that among other things he was a successful water dowser and he could "make a broom dance.'' Edgar explained that his father had an unusual attraction for snakes. They often would follow him home or wrap themselves around the brim of his hat when he left it in the field. ''It got on his nerves so much that he gave up farming'' (Thomas Sugrue, *There is a River*, New Dell Ed., p. 14).

As a child, Edgar was different from other boys in his behavior and interests. He became very fond of reading the Bible and enjoyed going to the Christian Church with his parents. Later he joined the church and was a Sunday School teacher. Edgar's son, Hugh, tells of the early signs of his father's psychic power:

> At the age of six or seven he told his parents that he was able to see and to talk to ''visions,'' sometimes of relatives who had recently died. . . . Later, by sleeping with his head on his schoolbooks, he developed some form of photographic memory which helped him advance rapidly in the country school. The gift faded [*Edgar Cayce on Healing*, pp. 8, 9].

By the age of fourteen he had read the entire Bible several times but he had difficulty in understanding it. He left school after completing the seventh grade and worked on a farm. After this he took a job in a shoestore and later he became a salesman for a wholesale stationery company. At this time he developed a paralysis of his throat muscles which defied medical diagnosis. The doctors could not find any physical explanation. Being unable to speak above a whisper for about a year, Cayce quit as a salesman and became an apprentice photographer.

Attempts to cure his throat problem by hypnosis failed, but on March 31, 1901, Cayce's friend, Al Layne, helped him to reenter the trance state he had achieved as a child and he was able to deal with his own problem: ''Speaking from an unconscious state, he recommended medication and manipulative therapy which successfully restored his voice and repaired his system" (ibid., p. 9). This was Cayce's first "reading." From this time until his death,

> it is estimated that he entered his sleep-like state at least 16,000 times during those years, although there is no way of definitely knowing the total. The earliest reading in the files dates back to 1909, but regular records were not kept on a systematic basis until Cayce's lifelong secretary, Gladys Davis, joined him in September 1923 [A.R.E. *Introductory Brochure*, p. 6]

Up until 1923 Cayce's *readings* continued to be primarily "physical readings." His trance information brought cures to hundreds and the newspapers picked up the story. It was in 1923 that Cayce was contacted at his photography business in Selma, Alabama, by Arthus Lammers. He was a wealthy printer from Dayton, Ohio, whose reason for visiting Cayce was different.

> He had other interests: philosophy, metapyhsics, esoteric astrology, psychic phenomena. He asked questions Edgar did not understand. . . . He mentioned such things as the cabala, the mystery religions of Egypt and Greece, the medieval alchemists, the mystics of Tibet, yoga, Madame Blavatsky and theosophy, the Great White Brotherhood, the Etheric World. Edgar was dazed [*There is a River*, p. 200].

Lammers wanted to check to see if the *readings* would confirm or deny his views. Lammers secured the first of the "life readings" (accounts of past earth lives) and his views on astrology and reincarnation were supported by the *readings*. At first, Cayce was disturbed when he was told what he had said while in trance.

> But what you've been telling me today, and what the readings have been saying, is foreign to all I've believed and been taught, and all I have taught to others, all my life. If ever the Devil was going to play a trick on me, this would be it [ibid., p. 210].

But instead of following this intuition, Cayce accepted Lammers' explanations on reincarnation and other matters and turned away from a literal interpretation of the Bible. Cayce's faith in the *readings* completed the transition. "Edgar Cayce had to reconcile reincarnation with his orthodox beliefs. He had to because he was confronted with the fact that the Readings didn't lie" (*The Searchlight,* Dec., 1958, p. 2).

At Lammer's invitation and with the promise of support, the Cayce family moved to Dayton, Ohio. But after business reverses, Lammers' financial support was dropped and in 1925 the Cayces moved to Virginia Beach, Virginia, in keeping with what the *readings* had indicated. In 1928 the Cayce Hospital for Research and Enlightenment was dedicated. It was lost during the Depression; repurchased in 1956, it now serves as the Headquarters of A.R.E.

Near the end of Cayce's life the requests for help which came were beyond him—some fifteen hundred a day. Although he was warned to cut down to two *readings* a day he did seven or eight and he burned himself out for "The Work." At the time of his death in 1945, the A.R.E. had less than seven hundred members. Edgar's son, Hugh Lynn, took over the organization when he returned after the war.

A.R.E. and the Edgar Cayce Foundation

In 1931 the Association for Research and Enlightenment, Inc., was founded in Virginia Beach, Virginia, replacing the Association of National Investigators, Inc. The announced purpose of A.R.E. was "to preserve, study and present the Edgar Cayce readings." In 1975 the paid membership of the Association was approaching 15,000, reaching 20,000 in 1980. Thousands of other people meet in about 1,600 "Search for God" groups in the United States and other countries. Additional thousands have become interested in Edgar Cayce through the dozens of books written about him and his *readings*. The books *There is a River* and *Edgar*

Cayce—the Sleeping Prophet were both high on best seller lists. Others like Hugh Cayce's *Venture Inward* and Noel Langley's *Edgar Cayce on Reincarnation* have gone through a number of printings.

Publications of the A.R.E. Press include the bimonthly *A.R.E. Journal,* the monthly *A.R.E. News, Treasure Trove* (a children's magazine), and hundreds of thousands of other pieces of literature including a number of substantial books and booklets. Further evidence of the growth of this group was the dedication of a new Library-Conference Center in 1975. The A.R.E. also holds workshops and conferences, runs summer youth camps, provides a book and tape library, offers courses through its Atlantic University, and maintains a clinic and medical division in Phoenix, Arizona.

The Edgar Cayce Foundation was established in 1947 and acts as the custodian of the original copies of the Edgar Cayce *readings* which are stored in a fireproof vault in the Headquarters building. Duplicate copies of the *readings* are available for study in the A.R.E. library.

The Edgar Cayce Readings

The Edgar Cayce "Readings" (a term used to describe the clairvoyant discourses which Edgar Cayce gave while in a self-induced hypnotic sleep-state) comprise a body of material of over 49,000 pages, which deals with a number of different topics. The *readings* have been cross-indexed on over 200,000 file cards.

The *readings* break down into several categories: 1) 8,985 "physical readings" (concerned with the mind and body); 2) 2,500 "life readings" (deal with accounts of past lives, vocational, psychological, and human relations problems); 3) 667 *readings* on dream interpretation; 4) "of the remaining 1,995, a rough breakdown would yield almost as many categories as there are readings" (A.R.E. *Introductory Brochure,* p. 6). Of the 2,500 "life readings," given for approximately 1,600 people, almost fifty percent had incarnations in the legendary Atlantis (Edgar Evans Cayce, *Edgar Cayce on Atlantis,* p. 27).

Edgar Cayce and Christian Doctrine

Those who write about Edgar Cayce do not question his honesty, sincerity, motives or humanitarian goals, but Bible-believing Christians reject his psychic readings because they are often diametrically opposed to orthodox Christianity. Acceptance of Cayce's psychic "enlightenment" requires a denial of the Person and Work of Jesus Christ as well as other Christian teachings. While A.R.E. officials state that the organization is "a study group and not a religion" (so this writer was told in his visit to Virginia Beach), the Cayce *readings* do present another "plan of salvation"—"another gospel" (Gal. 1:6-9). To the Christian, the core of Edgar Cayce is not his healings, but his theology which presents reincarnation as its central theme. Several examples from Cayce's readings and from books based on them will illustrate their erroneous and heretical nature.

The *readings* teach that Jesus was Adam and that he learned he would be the Savior "when he fell in Eden" (Reading 2067-7). According to the *readings* Jesus "possibly had some thirty incarnations during His development in becoming The Christ" (Jeffrey Furst, *Edgar Cayce's Story of Jesus,* pp. 76, 77).

The *readings* indicate that "much of the Bible can be interpreted either physically, mentally, or spiritually, and often on all levels simultaneously" (ibid., p. 79). Such an approach makes a shambles of sound exegesis. The *readings* also state that the Gospel of John "was written by several; not the John who was the Beloved . . ." and that "Luke was written by Lucius rather than Luke . . ." (ibid., p. 83). Lucius was Edgar Cayce in a previous incarnation who at that

126

time was a companion of Jesus Christ and the disciples (ibid., pp. 310-337).

Dr. Gina Cerminara's book *Many Mansions* ("The Edgar Cayce Story on Reincarnation"), with an introduction and high recommendation by Hugh Lynn Cayce, clearly illustrates the basic incompatibility of biblical Christianity and the Cayce *readings*.

> For almost twenty centuries the moral sense of the Western world has been blunted by a theology which teaches the vicarious atonement of sin through Christ, the Son of God. . . . It can be felt then that perhaps the personality called Jesus was different from us only in that he was closer to the central light than we are.

> Moreover, Christ's giving of his life that men might be free is no unique event in history; the study of comparative religions reveals other saviors, among other peoples, who suffered martyrdom and death. In our own Western culture, many idealists have given their lives willingly for humanity's sake. . . . But no one feels that their effort redeems us from effort, or that their sacrifice absolves us of our own personal guilt [p. 63].

Dr. Cerminara goes on to state that to demand belief in the deity of Christ and His vicarious atonement for salvation is not Christian, but the error of theologians, and that

> it is a psychological crime because it places responsibility for redemption on something external to the self; it makes salvation dependent on belief in the divinity of another person rather than on self-transformation through belief in one's own intrinsic divinity [ibid.].

The December 1958 A.R.E. *Searchlight* presented the Cayce substitute for the biblical doctrine of redemption.

> Original sin is our reason for being incarnated; we are here to overcome our karma and win perfection which brings us into eternal life with no more need to incarnate. This would be overcoming even as Jesus the Christ overcame.

There are over 100 quotations in the Bible on eternal

life. Now this could mean that there is a plan of redemption from sin, through many lives, through Jesus Christ who showed the way through His various incarnations—growth to perfection. Otherwise, each brand-new soul (for each man born) would be taking on a sin he didn't commit. Otherwise only those who followed Jesus Christ could be redeemed. Would a wise and Merciful Heavenly Father permit so many of His children to be unredeemed because of a circumstantial date in history or an accident of geography? [p. 4].

In place of a basically Christian theology or philosophy, Cayce's *readings* present rather "a Christianized version of the mystery religions of ancient Egypt, Chaldea, Persia, India, and Greece . . ." (*There is a River*, p. 305).

Reincarnation and the Bible. Space does not permit an extensive treatment on reincarnation which is refuted primarily by the Biblical doctrine of the Atonement.

Hebrews 1:3 strikes at the very heart of reincarnation which requires that each person purge his own sin through successive incarnations:

Who being the brightness of *his* glory, and the express image of his person, and upholding all things by the word of his power, when he had by himself purged our sins, sat down on the right hand of the Majesty on high.

This is a brief, yet comprehensive statement, of the work of Christ at His first Advent. It was Jesus Christ who purged or cleansed our sins, and in Him sin's penalty was fully discharged. He "sat down," which indicates that His work was completed. One is reminded of the words of the hymn:

There is a fountain filled with blood
Drawn from Immanuel's veins;
And sinners plunged beneath that flood,
Lose all their guilty stains.

The Epistle to the Hebrews also refutes reincarnation:

And as it is appointed unto men once to die, but after this the judgment: so Christ was once offered to bear the sins

128

of many; and unto them that look for him shall he appear the second time without sin unto salvation [9:27, 28].

First John 1:7 presents the precious truth that "the blood of Jesus Christ his Son cleanseth us from all sin." In John 10:28 Jesus tells us, "And I give unto them eternal life; and they shall never perish . . ."; and the Apostle Paul writes that "the wages of sin *is* death; but the gift of God *is* eternal life through Jesus Christ our Lord" (Rom. 6:23). Scripture offers no support for the doctrine of reincarnation. (See W. R. Martin's *The Kingdom of the Cults* [pp. 288-294] and J. S. Wright's *Man in the Process of Time* [pp. 138-149] for a further examination and refutation of reincarnation.)

Concluding Evaluation

While Edgar Cayce did not claim infallibility for his prophecies, Jess Stearn's book *Edgar Cayce—The Sleeping Prophet,* first published in 1967, did add stature to Cayce's image as a prognosticator. But Robert Somerlott was not too impressed with either Cayce's prophecies or Stearn's techniques.

> Although physicians may dismiss Cayce's psychic healing, it is supported by extensive testimony. His ESP, less well substantiated, remains interesting and worth further investigation. But in the field of precognition Cayce's record is a catastrophe, and one stands in awe of Stearn's achievement: seldom has a man been able to make so much out of so little. To verify the rambling, vaguely stated forecasts is to make bricks without straw and the results are the same—the prophecies hold up when glanced at, crumble when touched [pp. 266, 267].

> It would be a tedious waste of time to go through more of the prophecies and their purported fulfillment. . . . There are so many predictions and most of them are of such a general nature that one can be found—or stretched—to fit almost any event [p. 269].

Although the A.R.E. denies that Edgar Cayce was a spirit-

129

ualist, occult expert Dr. Kurt Koch classified him along with Harry Edwards as a spiritualistic healer (*Demonology, Past and Present*, p. 124). It is interesting that after reading the introduction of early spiritualist Andrew Jackson Davis' book, *Principles of Nature*, Cayce remarked, "This sounds so much like me it gives me the creeps" (*There is a River*, p. 288). There were many similarities. The diagnosis of disease and healing, prophecy and other features are all well known in spiritualism.

It is also significant that Edgar Cayce himself was well aware of the fact that the *readings* were often contrary to what he had learned, believed, and taught, based upon the Bible alone. Dr. John Warwick Montgomery concludes that in Edgar Cayce is to be found "a classic case of a 'seer' being in reality *blind:* the blind leading the blind" (*Principalities and Powers*, p. 126).

BIBLIOGRAPHY

Bjornstad, James. *Twentieth Century Prophecy*. Minneapolis, Minn.: Bethany Fellowship, Inc., 1969. Part II (pp. 75-151) presents a Christian analysis of Cayce.

Godwin, John. *Occult America*. New York: Doubleday and Co., 1972. See chapter 5, "The Heritage of Edgar Cayce."

Martin, Walter R. *The Kingdom of the Cults*. Minneapolis, Minn.: Bethany Fellowship, Inc., 1965. Deals with reincarnation from a Christian perspective, pp. 288-294.

Petersen, William J. *Those Curious New Cults*. New Canaan, Conn.: Keats Publishing, Inc., 1973. Chapter 4, "Edgar Cayce and the A.R.E.," is written from a Christian perspective. See also Petersen's article in the May 1972 issue of *Eternity*.

Somerlott, Robert. *"Here, Mr. Splitfoot": An Informal Exploration into Modern Occultism*. New York: The Viking Press, 1971. Edgar Cayce discussed, pp. 265-272.

Swihart, Phillip J. *Reincarnation: Edgar Cayce and the Bible*. Downers Grove: InterVarsity Press, 1975.

Wright, J. Stafford. *Man in the Process of Time*. Grand Rapids: Wm. B. Eerdmans Publishing Co., 1956. See chapter 13, "The Evidence for Reincarnation," written from a Christian perspective.

Publications Recommended by the A.R.E.

The books and booklets in support of Edgar Cayce and on his *readings* are too numerous to list. Their number increases annually. These include Edgar Cayce on: dreams, prophecy, karma and reincarnation, ESP, Atlantis, religion, diet and health, the Dead Sea Scrolls, and Jesus. Works recommended for study by A.R.E. include: *There is a River* (Sugrue); *Edgar Cayce—Man of Miracles* (Millard); *Edgar Cayce—the Sleeping Prophet* (Stearn); *Many Mansions* and *The World Within* (Cerminara); *Venture Inward* (H. L. Cayce); *A Search for God* (books 1 and 2); *Edgar Cayce and Group Dynamics* (Kidd) and *Edgar Cayce on Religion and Psychic Experience* (Bro). All are available from A.R.E. Headquarters.

15

Sun Myung Moon and the Unification Church

Before Rev. Sun Myung Moon's "Day of Hope" tour in 1972, few Americans had ever heard of the Korean evangelist or the Holy Spirit Association for the Unification of World Christianity, commonly called the Unification Church. Moon claimed that he was speaking in America because God had commissioned him to do so on January 1, 1972. In this tour Rev. Moon spoke in seven major American cities, but what brought him into the national limelight were the full-page ads which were placed in newspapers in October, 1973, calling for Americans to unite in support of President Nixon. Moon's "Answer to Watergate" message called for Americans to "Forgive, love" and "unite." The 1973 and 1974 "Day of Hope" speaking tours took Moon to sixty-one cities. His speech at Madison Square Garden on September 18, 1974, attended by over 25,000 persons, marked the culmination of three years of speaking to the American people.

Currently the Unification Church claims two million followers worldwide and it is estimated that thirty thousand of these are in the United States. A survey of the newspapers and magazines which have treated the activities of Moon's

Unification Church indicates that beyond the gaining of converts the movement has provoked much controversy, speculation and suspicion, as well as some strong opposition. Who is Rev. Sun Myung Moon? What are the teachings of Moon and his Unification Church? Only a cursory examination of these questions is given here, but sources for further information are listed in the Selective Bibliography.

Sun Myung Moon and the Origin of the Unification Church

Sun M. Moon was born in North Korea in 1920. His parents were members of the Presbyterian Church, which is the largest Protestant denomination in Korea. He attended high school in Seoul. Moon relates how he often withdrew for prayer, and on Easter Morning in 1936 he claims that Jesus Christ appeared to him and told him " 'to carry out my unfinished task.' Then a voice from heaven said, 'You will be the completer of man's salvation by being the second coming of Christ' " (*A.D.*, May, 1974, p. 33). He did not begin his preaching ministry at that time, but studied and prepared himself for his mission. He went to Japan and studied electrical engineering at Waseda University in Tokyo. In 1944 he returned to his home in Korea and in 1946 founded the Broad Sea Church. He was excommunicated from the Presbyterian Church for his heretical teachings. For six months Moon attached himself to a community in South Korea called the Monastery of Israel, "learning what was to become the basis of his own theology, the 'Divine Principle' " (ibid.). After his return to North Korea he was arrested by the Communists and imprisoned for several years. Unification Church accounts indicate that Moon's years in prison were years of great suffering, and that his arrest and incarceration were because of his Christian stand and his anti-Communist activities. But "it is also widely believed in Korea that the immediate cause of his arrest was adultery. Moon had divorced his first wife to whom he was legally married and was twice remarried" (*Missiology,* July, 1975, p. 360).

Church and fortune established in South Korea: After he was freed by United Nations forces late in 1950, he returned to South Korea with some of his disciples and settled in Pusan. In 1954 he founded the Holy Spirit Association for the Unification of World Christianity—in reality a radical departure from Biblical Christianity. In the years that followed Rev. Moon built a network of industries and a personal fortune often estimated at fifteen million dollars. Because of his anti-Communist stance he enjoyed a privileged relationship with President Park's regime, and on June 7, 1975, over a million who gathered in Seoul heard Rev. Moon speak against Communism at the World Rally for Korean Freedom.

U.S. activities: In 1959 Miss Young Oon Kim was sent to the United States as the Unification Church's first missionary, where she established Unification centers and prepared an English adaptation of *Divine Principle* entitled *The Divine Principle and Its Application.* Since 1972 the Unification Church has acquired millions of dollars worth of property, much of it in the state of New York (Tarrytown, Barrytown, Irvington and Greenburg) as well as in Oklahoma, California, Louisiana and Washington. The church now has centers in all fifty states where members are busy soliciting converts and money. Through the Collegiate Association for the Research of Principles (or CARP—which has even appropriated the Christian fish symbol), the "Moonies" have been able to recruit a number of college students on campuses across America.

One writer stated that the Unification Church is "now probably the most active new Christian movement in the United States" and that its impact was not only being felt on the East and West Coasts, but also in the traditionally conservative Midwest (ibid., p. 359). Its efficient organization, financial strength, anti-Communist stance, youth orientation, missionary spirit and dedicated membership would seem to indicate that the Unification Church is a cult with which Christians must be prepared to contend.

The Teachings of Rev. Moon and the Unification Church

Character of theology: A study of such Unification Church publications as *Divine Principle* and *Divine Principle and Its Application*, along with *Unification Theology and Christian Thought* by Dr. Young Oon Kim, professor of systematic theology and world religions at Unification Theological Seminary, will quickly convince the Christian reader that this church represents a radical departure from "the faith" (Jude 3, 4). How has the Unification Church and its theology been characterized? Dean Peerman stated that it was

> a strange amalgam of Oriental family worship, Eastern religious teachings, spiritism, and dubious interpretations of history and Christianity [*Christian Century,* Dec. 4, 1974, p. 1139].

Robert S. Ellwood, Jr., said that the movement

> has all the marks of a Far Eastern new religion of the Japanese type. It has . . . strong traces of the traditional shamanism of the Korean countryside as well as of missionary Christianity; it places no small emphasis on clairvoyance, clairaudience, healing, and spiritualistic phenomena. Believers feel spiritual fire and electricity, and communicate mediumistically with spirits, Jesus and God [*Religious and Spiritual Groups in Modern America,* p. 292].

A *Time* magazine writer concluded:

> In essence, Moon's theology makes wide use of Biblical personae and events, but is no more than nominally Christian. Added ingredients are an odd mix: occultism, electrical engineering, Taoist dualism, pop sociology and opaque metaphysical jargon [Sept. 30, 1974, p. 69].

Quotations and Scriptural refutations: Moon's Unification Church theology is one of denial or perversion of all the major doctrines of historic Biblical Christianity. Ten examples are given here, together with suggested Scriptural refutations.

• *He teaches that his "New Truth" supersedes the Bible:* "It may be displeasing to religious believers, especially to Christians, to learn that a new expression of truth must appear. They believe that the Bible, which they now have, is perfect and absolute in itself" (*Divine Principle*, 2nd ed., 1973, p. 9. Key doctrinal authority of the Unification Church, hereafter referred to as DP). ". . . The New Testament words of Jesus and the Holy Spirit will lose their light. . . . To 'lose their light' means that the period of their mission has elapsed with the coming of the new age" (DP, p. 118). "Until our mission with the Christian Church is over, we must quote the Bible and use it to explain the Divine Principle. After we receive the inheritance of the Christian Church we will be free to teach without the Bible" (MS-7, p. l. MS is used as the abbreviation for "The Master Speaks"—questions and answers transcribed from tapes taken when Rev. Moon visited the U.S. in March and April 1965). (Isa. 40:8; Matt. 24:35; Mark 13:31; II Tim. 3:16; I Pet. 1:23-25)

• *He denies the virgin birth of Jesus Christ:* "Jesus was born of a father and a mother, just as anyone else is, but in this case the Spirit of God was working also" (MS-7, p. 4). "Modern theologians deny completely any supernatural birth for Jesus. They say Jesus had two parents. Conservatives say that he was born of the Holy Spirit without a human father. In our explanation we can reconcile these two extremely different positions" (MS-7, p. 5). (Matt. 1:18-20, 25; Luke 1:34, 35)

• *He denies the deity of Jesus Christ:* Although Moon speaks of Jesus as "God" and as "deity," these words do not convey orthodox meaning when understood. Twice, concerning Jesus, it is stated: ". . . He can by no means be God Himself" (DP, pp. 210, 211). After quoting John 8:58 it is stated: ". . . This also does not signify that Jesus was God Himself. Jesus, on earth, was a man no different from us except for the fact that he was without original sin" (DP, p. 212). "But after his crucifixion, Christianity made Jesus into God. This is why a gap between God and man has never been bridged" (*Christianity in Crisis*, pp. 12, 13). (John 1:1, 20:28; Heb. 1:6-12; Tit. 2:13; II Pet. 1:1)

● *He denies that the death of Christ on the cross was God's will:* "We, therefore, must realize that Jesus did not come to die on the cross" (DP, p. 143). ". . . We can see that Jesus' crucifixion was the result of the ignorance and disbelief of the Jewish people and was not God's predestination to fulfill the whole purpose of Jesus' coming as the Messiah" (DP, p. 145). Therefore, Jesus' ministry is viewed as a partial failure because it did not provide physical salvation—only spiritual. (Mark 10:45; Luke 24:25, 26; John 17:4; I Cor. 15:3; Col. 1:20-22; Heb. 9:26; 10:14)

● *He denies the bodily resurrection of Jesus Christ:* Moon was asked, "Was Jesus' physical body resurrected?" His answer, "No. Jesus no longer needed the physical body" [MS-4 (2), p. 9]. (Luke 24:39; Acts 2:27-32; 13:33-37; Rom. 8:11)

● *He denies the Second Coming of Christ as taught in Acts 1:9-11:* ". . . Although many Christians up to the present have believed that Jesus would come on the clouds, there are no grounds to deny the possibility of the Lord being born in the flesh on the earth at the Second Advent . . ." (DP, pp. 500, 501). (Acts 1:11; I Thess. 4:15-17; Rev. 1:7)

● *He perverts the Biblical account of the fall of man:* ". . . Man fell because of fornication. . . . Both man and angel [Satan] fell because of fornication" (DP, pp. 72, 73). As a result of this "illicit blood relationship" Adam and Eve "could not multiply the good lineage of God, but rather

137

multiplied the evil lineage of Satan'' (DP, p. 75). (Gen. 2:16, 17; 3:1-12)

● *He teaches the abolition of hell and the universal reconciliation of all, including Satan:* ''The ultimate purpose of God's providence is to save all mankind. Therefore, it is God's intention to abolish Hell completely, after the lapse of the period necessary for the full payment of all indemnity'' (DP, p. 190). ''. . . Even evil spirits . . . will take part in the fulfillment of God's will'' (DP, p. 191). ''Will he [Satan] be restored completely?'' Moon's answer, ''Of course. But it will take almost an eternity for it to happen. He has a great deal of indemnity to pay'' (MS-6, p. 4). (Matt. 25:41, 46; II Thess. 1:7-10; Heb. 9:27; Rev. 20:10)

● *He claims to have had contact with the spirit world and engages in spiritualism:* In his book *Unknown but Known* (pp. 111, 112), the late Arthur Ford included an account of a seance at which Rev. Moon was present. The communication through ''Fletcher,'' Ford's control, confirmed Moon's mission. Unification Church members are told that ''even without contacting the spirit world, our Leader can control mediums. When a medium reports to him, he knows which part of the message is correct and which part is incorrect and what advice he would give to the medium'' [MS-4 (2), p. 10]. Young Oon Kim stated that, ''Some members came to this group through direct guidance of the spirit world. The Blessed Mother Mary, Gautama Buddha, and Confucius are among those in the spirit world who are directing certain of their followers to this group'' (*Divine Principle and Its Application*, p. x). (Lev. 19:31; 20:6, 27; Deut. 18:10-12; Isa. 8:19, 20)

● *He teaches that he is the Messiah, the Lord of the Second Advent:* Since he began his ministry to America it has been difficult to establish definitely that Moon considered himself to be the new Messiah. Jane D. Mook, in agreement with other writers, stated that ''in the early days of the movement he admitted that he did consider himself the Messiah'' (*A.D.*, May, 1974, p. 34). Wi Jo Kang, who authored an article on the Unification Church, noted that all the members of the movement who answered his questions ''also confessed that they truly believe that Rev. Mr. Moon is the Messiah'' (*Missiology*, July, 1975, p. 368). A confirmation that Moon currently claims to be the Messiah is given by *L.A. Times* reporter John Dart. In a confidential Unification Church training manual examined by the reporter, Moon is referred to as ''Father,'' ''Master,'' and ''Messiah'' (Jan. 29, 1976, p. 3) (Matt. 24:23-27).

Author's Conclusions

In ending this brief treatment, this writer is reminded of two passages of Scripture. The first is Mark 13:5, 6, which finds its fulfillment in men like Rev. Moon. The other is I Timothy 4:1—especially appropriate in its application because of Moon's admitted contacts with spiritualism:

> Now the Spirit speaketh expressly, that in the latter times some shall depart from the faith, giving heed to seducing spirits, and doctrines of devils [demons].

BIBLIOGRAPHY

Austin, Charles M. ''Sun Myung Moon,'' *Christian Herald*, Dec., 1974, pp. 14-16, 19, 20.

Bjornstad, James. *The Moon is Not the Son*. Minneapolis: Bethany Fellowship, 1976.

Ellwood, Robert S. *Religious and Spiritual Groups in Modern America*. Prentice-Hall, 1973, pp. 291-295.

Ferraro, Susan. ''Trouble in Tarrytown,'' *New York Sunday News*, July 20, 1975, pp. 14-16.

Kang, Wi Jo. ''The Influence of the Unification Church in the United States of America,'' *Missiology, An International Review*, July, 1975, pp. 357-368.

Levitt, Zola. *The Spirit of Sun Myung Moon*. Irvine, Calif.: Harvest House Publishers, 1976.

Mook, Jane Day. "New Growth on Burnt-Over Ground III: the Unification Church," *A.D.*, May, 1975, pp. 32-36.

Yamamoto, J. Isamu. *The Moon Doctrine*. Downers Grove: InterVarsity Press, 1976.

———. *The Puppet Master*. Downers Grove: InterVarsity Press, 1977.

A number of short treatments and reports on the Unification Church have appeared in *Time, Newsweek, The Christian Century* and *Christianity Today*.

For a study of Unification Church theology, *Divine Principle* and *Divine Principle and Its Application* are essential. *Unification Theology and Christian Thought* by Dr. Young Oon Kim gives a more academic approach. A good summary of some of the main ideas of Unification theology is presented in Moon's Madison Square Garden speech published as an advertisement in major newspapers such as the *L.A. Times*, Dec. 24, 1974, "The New Future of Christianity."

In the study document, "A Critique of the Theology of the Unification church as Set Forth in 'Divine Principle' " (*Occasional Bulletin*, July, 1977, pp. 18-23), prepared by the Commission on Faith and Order of the National Council of Churches, the following conclusions were stated:

A. The Unification Church is not a Christian Church.
  1. Its doctrine of the nature of the Triune God is erroneous.
  2. Its Christology is incompatible with Christian teaching and belief.
  3. Its teaching on salvation and the means of grace is inadequate and faulty.

B. The claims of the Unification Church to Christian identity cannot be recognized.
  1. The role and authority of Scripture are compromised in the teachings of the Unification Church.
  2. Revelations are invoked as divine and normative in *Divine Principle* which contradict basic elements of Christian faith.

3. A 'new, ultimate, final truth' is presented to complete and supplant all previously recognized religious teachings, including those of Christianity (p. 23).

In addition to those mentioned in this article, Sun Myung Moon's Front Organizations include: Project Unity, One World Crusade, International Cultural Foundation, International Federation for Victory Over Communism, Freedom Leadership Foundation, World Freedom Institute, Little Angels of Korea, Professors Academy for World Peace, Unified Family, International Re-Education Foundation, American Youth for a Just Peace, Korean Folk Ballet, New Hope Singers International, Committee for Responsible Dialogue, International Conference on Unified Science and the C.D.C. Striders Track Club. The total is over forty.

16

The Christian in an Age of Confusion

Astrologers tell us that our age is characterized by a new religious atmosphere. While a person may be skeptical concerning astrologers and astrology, he cannot ignore the popularity and increasing influence of many cults (both old and new). Religions imported from the Far East and cults of many kinds seem to be flourishing. One can venture almost anywhere in America and find evidence of, and even sometimes an obsession with, cultism and the occult. From all appearances the trend will continue and perhaps even accelerate. We certainly find ourselves in a new religious atmosphere, but unfortunately it is often characterized by religious deception and the outright rejection of Biblical Christianity.

In this age of religious and occult confusion many people have discontinued the search for ultimate truth as a hopeless quest. A number of others have concluded that religious truth could not be found easily, and they became confirmed "truth seekers": "Ever learning, and never able to come to the knowledge [recognition] of the truth" (II Tim. 3:7). Some of these "seekers" actually resisted the truth and others did not recognize their need and the redemption provided by Jesus Christ.

The Bible-believing Christian cannot accept the popular statement that "*all* religions lead to the same place." Instead, he accepts the Bible's promise that one *can know the truth,* for ultimate TRUTH is not a system—an "it"—but a *Person,* Jesus Christ ("I am . . . the truth," John 14:6). Truth to the Christian is also conformity to the revealed will of God as set forth in the Bible. "To the law and to the testimony: if they speak not according to this word, *it is* because *there is* no light in them" (or, "they have no dawn," NASB, i.e., *no future hope,* Isa. 8:20). "Every human opinion, religion, or philosophy is valid only as it agrees with God's Word—the only absolute yardstick of spiritual truth" (Gleason L. Archer, Jr., "Isaiah," *The Wycliffe Bible Commentary,* p. 619).

Paul's admonition to Timothy and the predicted apostasy which would reach its culmination in the present age is essential reading for the Christian:

> Preach the word: be instant in season, out of season; reprove, rebuke, exhort with all long-suffering and doctrine. For the time will come when they will not endure sound doctrine; but after their own lusts shall they heap to themselves teachers, having itching ears; and they shall turn away *their* ears from the truth, and shall be turned unto fables [II Tim. 4:2-4].

The believer in Christ is to "preach [herald] the word," the Gospel, message of redemption in Jesus Christ. Why must the Christian be diligent in preaching, reproving, rebuking and exhorting? Because the time when "they will not endure sound doctrine" is at hand. "Sound doctrine" is that doctrine which promotes spiritual health. Instead many men crave and acquire teachers who preach and teach that which suits their perverted appetites. People are often more interested in something different, sensational, fascinating and

143

philosophical, than in the truth. As a result, in turning away from the truth they "turned unto fables" (see: I Tim. 1:4; 4:7; Tit. 1:14). This description well characterizes the situation of many of those who are in the cults and the occult today.

Testing Religious Teachings

In addition to exposing doctrinal error through teaching and preaching "all the counsel of God" (Acts 20:27), it is helpful for the Christian to have a series of questions by which he might examine and test the teachings of those groups with which he comes in contact. The following list could be expanded, but these questions will assist the Christian in his attempt to discern truth from error. Some will apply to certain groups and not to others.

- What is their attitude toward the Person of Jesus Christ: Do they hold to His incarnation; do they accept His Deity?
- Do they believe in a personal God and accept the Trinity?
- Do they believe in the bodily resurrection of Christ?
- Do they alter the Bible by adding to or subtracting from it? Do they follow the Bible for doctrinal authority? Do they study the Bible as a whole?
- Do they base their doctrines on the plain and direct statements of the Bible? Is their doctrinal foundation that of types, parables, figures of speech, prophecy, etc.?
- Are their main doctrinal points based on the Old Testament? On the New Testament? Do they place their organization in the events of Revelation after the third chapter at the present time?
- Do they exalt human leaders? Are these leaders and/or the organizations they represent deemed essential for the understanding of the Bible? For their salvation?
- Do they see man as a helpless sinner?
- Is their approach to God and salvation on the basis of works or grace?
- Do they believe in the conscious punishment of the lost?

144

Do they believe in the judgment to come? Do they believe in a second chance?

These questions are only suggestions as to what might be asked. Others should be added and Scriptures be compiled for each. (For a helpful list of Scripture references see Keith L. Brooks' *Rock Foundations of Truth*.) The Christian also should discuss what the adherents of any group mean by the terms which they use. (For a good discussion on the problem of semantics see Walter Martin's *The Kingdom of the Cults*, chapter 2.)

In dealing with the followers of a cult or other non-Christian belief these two questions are vital: 1) What is the basis of their personal relationship to God? 2) To what extent do they have assurance of salvation as a present possession? I John 5:10-13 presents the heart of the Gospel message and the standard for these two vital questions.

> He that believeth on the Son of God hath the witness in himself: he that believeth not God hath made him a liar; because he believeth not the record that God gave of his Son. And this is the record, that God hath given to us eternal life, and this life is in his Son. He that hath the Son hath life; *and* he that hath not the Son of God hath not life. These things have I written unto you that believe on the name of the Son of God; that ye may know that ye have eternal life, and that ye may believe on the name of the Son of God.

Reaching the Lost in Cult and Occult Confusion

Many Christians are pessimistic concerning the fruitfulness of time spent in attempting to reach persons involved in the cults and the occult. Are such attempts worth the effort? Can these people be reached? The answer to both of these questions is **yes.** One will find that a number of recently published books give or contain the personal testimonies of conversion from non-Christian involvements. *We Found Our Way Out* (Baker Book, 1964), gives the testimonies of persons who were delivered from a number of the cults as well as from such diverse backgrounds as Satanism and Communism. *I Talked With Spirits* (Tyndale House, 1970) and *The Challenging Counterfeit* (Logos, 1966) both include accounts of conversion from spiritualism. *Mormonism—Shadow or Reality?* (Modern Microfilm, 1972 ed.) is only one of dozens of excellent works written by Jerald and Sandra Tanner, converts from Mormonism. *The Satan Seller* (Logos, 1972) was written by a former Satanist high priest. Roberta Blankenship wrote of her experiences in *Escape From Witchcraft* (Zondervan, 1972). *Death of a Guru* (Holman, 1977) is an autobiography of a convert from Hinduism. *We Left Jehovah's Witnesses* (Presbyterian and Reformed, 1974) presents the experiences and salvation testimonies of six couples. "Cult Explosion" (New Liberty Enterprises, 1979), is a powerful film which gives the testimonies of converts from a number of the cults. The list of similar stories of deliverance could be multiplied many times.

An experience which is still continuing should be an encouragement to every Christian to be active in his witness for Christ to those in religious and occult confusion. The beginning of this story goes back to the year 1957 when seventeen-year-old Ken Guindon was baptized as a Jehovah's Witness. In 1958 he began 14 years of full-time service with the movement. This led him from his home in California to Maine, then to Brooklyn, New York; and after graduation from the Watchtower Bible School of Gilead, to the Ivory Coast as a missionary. Ken and his wife Monique were led by circumstances to return to the United States at the end of 1971.

In a letter dated March 16, 1973, the Guindons submitted their resignation to their local Kingdom Hall. What had brought them to this decision? It resulted from the faithful testimonies of ordinary Christians who showed by their lives and their witness that Jesus Christ did make a difference. Ken was challenged by these dedicated Christians and he began a personal in-depth study of the Bible. He shared what he found with his wife. He read Christian books, attended meetings, and consulted with born-again Christians. Both Ken and his wife invited Jesus Christ into their hearts as their Lord and Savior and accepted salvation as a *gift* (Eph. 2:8, 9). A short time later both were baptized.

Since Ken's conversion he has led many people to Christ including another Witness couple, Douglas and Barbara Wiskow. They had studied with the Witnesses for several years and Douglas had been baptized. On October 18, 1973, he accepted Christ and his wife made the same decision the next day. A letter of resignation was sent to the Kingdom Hall a week later. The Wiskows, now free in Christ (cf. Gal. 5:1), shared their faith with relatives who also accepted Christ and left their Witness involvement. This is a continuing account, for both the Guindons and the Wiskows are committed to reaching others for Jesus Christ. The Wiskows were also baptized in testimony of the finished work of Christ in their lives. Ken began his *full-time* ministry of reaching cultists and the lost for Christ less than one year after his conversion. God certainly blesses the faithful testimonies of dedicated Christians and the results continue through this life and throughout eternity!*

Is it worth the time and effort to attempt to reach cultists and those involved in the occult? Again, *yes it is!* This writer was also won to Christ from the Jehovah's Witnesses as a result of the faithful testimony of his teen-age friends. They were not well-trained in the Scriptures, but they did know Christ as a living reality in their lives. Thank God for those who share their Christian faith in the Age of Aquarius—an age of religious and occult confusion!

---

*The Guindon's testimony is included in the book *We Left Jehovah's Witnesses* (Presbyterian and Reformed, Baker Book House). Ken and Monique are presently missionaries in France.

Appendix

Some Christian Countercult Resource Organizations

Bill Parker (Acts 17, Box 2183, La Mesa, Calif. 92041) has prepared a comprehensive "Index to Countercult Resources" which lists "nearly every Christian non-periodical publication available on cults" and the publishers, organizations or individuals where these may be obtained.

The following is a selective list of organizations which deal with a number of cults rather than those which specialize. Publications are given in parentheses. Other particulars concerning: catalogs, literature, tapes, speakers, research, etc., should be obtained through contact with each organization.

Christian Apologetics: Research and Information
   Service (CARIS)
P.O. Box 1783
Santa Ana, Calif. 92702
(Newsletter)

Christian Research Institute
P.O. Box 500
San Juan Capistrano, Calif. 92675
(*Forward*)

Institute of Contemporary Christianity
Box A
Oakland, New Jersey 07436
(*Contemporary Christianity*)

Jesus People USA
4707 N. Malden
Chicago, Ill. 60640
(*Cornerstone*—contains articles on the cults)

Spiritual Counterfeits Project
P.O. Box 4308
Berkeley, Calif. 94704
(*Newsletter,* annual *SCP Journal*)

Religion Analysis Service
2708 E. Lake Street, Suite 231
Minneapolis, Minn. 55406
(*The Discerner*)